MY MOTHER'S MURDER

GINA JANE HAMILTON MCGAVIN

MIRROR BOOKS

MB

MIRROR BOOKS

© Gina McGavin

The rights of Gina McGavin to be identified as the author of this book have been asserted, in accordance with the Copyright, Designs and Patents Act 1988.

All rights reserved. No part of this publication may be reproduced, stored in a retrieval system, or transmitted, in any form or by any means without the prior written permission of the publisher, nor be otherwise circulated in any form of binding or cover other than that in which it is published and without a similar condition being imposed on the subsequent purchaser.

1

Written with Jane Hamilton

Published in Great Britain and Ireland in 2025 by Mirror Books, a Reach PLC business.

www.mirrorbooks.co.uk
@TheMirrorBooks

Print ISBN 9781917439084
eBook ISBN 9781917439077

Cover Design: Chris Collins
Editing and Production: Christine Costello

Every effort has been made to trace copyright.
Any oversight will be rectified in future editions.

Printed and bound in Great Britain by
CPI Group (UK) Ltd, Croydon, CR0 4YY

*This book is dedicated to the memory of my mum
Mary Ann McLaughlin nee Murphy,
affectionately known as 'Wee Mary'*

'Arrivederci'

Contents

Foreword	9
Prologue	11
Author's Note	13
Mary Ann Murphy	16
Love and Marriage	33
A Glasgow Childhood	46
Wee Joe in The Drum	55
First Job and First Love	64
Marriage to Maryhill	75
Memories of my Mum	85
The Grim Reaper	98
A Callous Killer	111
The Hunters	130
Shame	146
A Whole Lot of Speculation	154
Kathleen	161
And The World Keeps Spinning	177
A Breath of Fresh Air	189
Diamonds and Pearls	197
The Weight of Alibis	202
A Cold Case Awakens	220

Breakthrough	232
Eureka	237
The Anatomy of Proof and Justice	243
Is Anybody Listening?	263
Letting Go And Embracing New Beginnings	280
Acknowledgements	285

Foreword

EMERITUS PROFESSOR DAVID WILSON

NO MURDERER should ever be allowed to keep the story of his victim to himself. And, more importantly, no murder victim should be reduced to a few headlines that spend more time discussing developments in forensic science that brought the culprit to justice, or the police's tenacity in pursuing the case, than describing the life of the person who died. The former hides in silence, the latter far too often in ebullient praise.

Who inevitably gets lost is the person who was killed – in all their idiosyncratic guises, strengths and weaknesses, foibles, and quirks. So, they are quickly reduced as a human being and repackaged to tell a re-assuring tale about the success of DNA, or how the police will eventually triumph over evil, and how the criminal justice system provides closure for the family who get left behind.

This beautifully written and consistently thoughtful book about the murder of Mary McLaughlin in 1984 is a corrective to this trend.

With a narrative that resembles a Russian doll, we discover Mary as a child, a mother, a grandmother and a murder victim and then the persistence of her daughter Gina to get justice for the woman who abandoned her as little girl.

It's a story of Glasgow, "the ordinary things that make up a life" and a search for the truth which refuses to "sit still". Above all, it's really the story of the strength and courage of Gina – one of those Glaswegian women who are too often ignored, belittled, and dismissed, but who are actually the backbone of Scotland.

This is true crime at its very best – evocative, haunting, and complex but with an overpowering sense of how the "slippery past" will eventually catch up with us all.

Prologue

ON OCTOBER 2, 1984, just three weeks after we buried my dad, I was busy preparing dinner for my family when the phone rang.

Expecting the caller to be my husband to say he was either on his way home or working late, I was surprised to hear the voice of one of my siblings. There had been animosity at Dad's funeral. I braced myself for an argument. Martin was upset. His voice was shaky. I felt a stirring of alarm.

"Gina, I have just been to my ma's, she's dead, she's been murdered."

Those words sent an icy chill through my body.

"The police are at my ma's flat now, when I went to her door, I didn't get an answer, I looked through the letterbox. The lights and the central heating were on. The smell was so bad I knew that something was very wrong. I kicked the door in and I found her body."

His words weren't sinking in. I was silent while my brain scrambled to process what he had just said. Then shock kicked in and I went into automatic pilot mode. Think, Gina, think!

I couldn't leave the children alone, my husband worked 10 minutes from our house and often stopped at the bookies on his way home. I needed to catch him before he left. Luckily, I did. The thought of traipsing to a bookies to find my wayward husband to tell him such news was more than I could stand, so I phoned instead. I needed to catch him before he left. Luckily, I did. I had, in my head, rehearsed what I was going to say – something gentle and not too dramatic.

When my husband came to the phone the first words that came out my mouth were, "Mum has been murdered. You have to come straight home."

Whoever thinks they're going to have to tell people their mum was murdered?

Little did I know, I would spend decades saying it.

Author's Note

AS YOU read this book, you may wonder why I bothered to fight for a woman I barely knew. A woman who abandoned all of her children in pursuit of a happiness that proved as unreliable as she was.

Even though she was dead, I felt strongly that I had to make a connection with Mary and try to understand her.

I wanted to put everything I know about her, such as it is, into perspective and for over 35 years to put myself in her place and imagine how her life must have been, the upbringing that shaped her, the choices she made and the reasons behind her decision to abandon 11 children when they needed her the most.

For many years I asked myself why she would leave us. Even now, thoughts and fears of abandonment creep up from the darkest recesses of my mind leaving me feeling angry and resentful. But then I feel guilty and remember she was a human being who was just as flawed as we all are. We all make mistakes, some more than others and some we are destined to repeat over and over again.

I have constant battles in my own mind about why I continued to fight for her and why I have a deep love for a woman I called 'Mother' but who I never really knew.

As a child I longed for her, as an adult I grieved for her.

I have spent more than half my life searching for answers and seeking the truth – often to the detriment of my own health and wellbeing but this is something I have felt driven to do.

I feel people need to know her whole story and not just 'Mary McLaughlin, murder victim.'

You will read this book and consider if she was a nice person, a good person, a 'worthy' victim and you will wonder how she could walk out on her family not just once, but twice.

I firmly believe my mum was born in a time when post-natal depression was not recognised.

Mary suffered after her children were born and did not have the means or the support to 'just get over' the so-called baby blues.

With no family to lean on and without any experience herself of a stable home life, how could she be expected to be a steady influence on anyone else?

I have tried to be as honest as possible; I have fragmented memories of my mother but I reminisce about

AUTHOR'S NOTE

the few times we met and had conversations. Some of those are tinged with sadness but others I look back on and find them humorous. She was a funny person and she loved to make you laugh. I hope that comes through in some of my recollections of her.

She lived on this planet for just 58 years and she died a horrible, painful death.

I cannot forget that. Regardless of what she did or how she treated the people in her life.

She was a woman born in the wrong time and she paid a heavy price for that.

Above all, Mary Ann McLaughlin was a human being who did not deserve to die the way she did.

This is a story about the past, the present and the future.

It's a story about two women who longed for maternal love they never fully experienced and looked for it elsewhere.

It's a story about love, grief, justice and hope.

Mary Ann Murphy Mullen McLaughlin.

This is her story.

1

Mary Ann Murphy

At their core, all tales, both real and imagined, are rooted in some truth.

But Cinderella, a fairy tale spun from the imaginations of storytellers, held a little too much truth for Mary Ann Murphy. Its narrative mirrored her own reality in a very unsettling way.

The start of Mary's life seemed so different. She was born out of love to two parents who were happily married. They lived in Glasgow in their own little bubble.

She was nurtured and adored by her mother who was devoted to the young Mary.

But tragedy was just around the corner.

Kathleen Murphy succumbed to tuberculosis at the tender age of 23 leaving behind a bereft, grief-stricken husband and a confused five-year-old child who spent months crying out for her mother.

Unable to cope, George Murphy foisted the care of his child onto his sisters.

They were stone-hearted women with little affection or sympathy for the child who had been forced on them.

They weren't shy about making their feelings known – to her at least.

My mother never experienced the carefree joys of childhood. Her earliest memories were not of comfort but of absence. Her mother died when she was still young enough to forget her face but old enough to feel the hollow Kathleen's death left behind.

The aunts, sharp-handed women, took her in out of duty not love and treated her like an orphan.

There was bitterness about another child to look after, another mouth to feed.

There was no kindness or love for Mary and it would be a pattern that would follow her for most of her life.

She would carry that ache – of love withheld – and a childhood 'stolen' for the rest of her life. But she would carry it on her own terms because in a city that tried to forget girls like her, Mary remembered herself.

To understand my mother and the woman she became, we need to go back to her beginning.

Mary Ann Murphy was born on May 22, 1926.

Her father was a merchant seaman and was often gone for long periods of time. Instead of seeking comfort with his child he used his job as an escape from his grief. Besides, it wasn't on a man's radar to take care of children – it was the duty of women to care for the children while the men worked and brought home the money.

And so George decided his child would live with his sisters and he would send them money when he could.

Mary's well being and upbringing was left to the two women. Mary was an obligation, not a joy. A tiresome, unwanted burden. The sisters showed their resentment by abusing her both physically and mentally.

They refused to support the child and made her work for everything. Can you imagine being told at just five years old by those who are supposed to love you and keep you safe that you needed to earn your keep? That if you wanted to eat you had to work hard for it.

Mary was given a long list of chores that would probably seem overwhelming to an adult never mind a child. If the chores weren't carried out to their satisfaction, she was made to repeat them over and over again until she got it right. Children that age are still learning how to dress themselves and brush their teeth but Mary was expected to make beds, scrub floors, wash dishes, clean windows, peel potatoes and anything else they could think of to keep her busy when she wasn't at school.

Whenever the mood took the aunts, Mary was beaten.

In her later years, my mother rarely spoke of this time in her life. The pain was too great. I always say she wore a 'painted smile' as an adult and it wasn't until I heard of her childhood that I realised exactly why I thought this. Deep down inside, my mother was very unhappy and used humour and laughter to disguise that.

Her young cousin, Elsie, who also lived in the house, soon realised that the timid and shy Mary was an easy target and could be blamed for everything.

"Mary turned the bedroom light on," she told the aunts. Slap! Right across her face.

"Mary didn't make the bed!" Another slap. And on it went.

If Mary tried to defend herself, she was told she was an insolent naughty child. That nobody wanted her.

Whenever her father returned from sea and brought her toys they would be taken from her and given to her cousins who would break them. Mary would be smacked by her father when he found out the toys he was spending his hard-earned money on were broken. He was never told Mary didn't actually get to play with them.

Life was hard for her. There was no respite or escape from the abuse she was forced to endure. Sporadic visits from her father didn't help. He wasn't interested in her suffering. In fact, it was probably a relief to him that his daughter was someone else's problem. The only time he showed an interest in Mary was when she was being punished.

Life for children in Glasgow in the 1920s and 1930s

was forged in the shadows of industry, smoke-stained tenements, and grinding poverty. On paper, the city was booming. Its skyline was dominated by cranes and chimneys, but beneath the hum of industrial progress, working-class families and children knew little beyond how to survive day to day. It was an often brutal existence. The city's thriving industry meant nothing to the children growing up in the tenements and slums.

The days would begin early with the sounds of milk carts and bellows of a factory horn calling men to their shifts in the shipyards and factories – if they were lucky enough to have work.

By the 1930s the Great Depression had hit Glasgow hard. Thousands of men were idly twiddling their thumbs, queuing up for jobs that didn't exist or lined up for relief payments such as they were. Poor relief, it was called. But it wasn't much. And you would often only get it if the man from the welfare said you didn't have anything in the house to sell.

Women stretched their flour, lard and worries as far as they could go.

Families would be cramped in single rooms or kitchen flats and there was little privacy or comfort. Breakfast was a luxury and children would start their days without it more often than not. If there was any breakfast to be had, it was usually a slice of bread with dripping or lard – animal fat skimmed from cheap cuts of meat –

sometimes there was watery porridge stretched to feed many mouths. Meat for dinner was extremely rare, and dinner would often be no more than a slice of bread. Children knew more about hunger than they did about play.

The Scottish weather was relentless and unpredictable. The cold was a constant presence.

Coal was expensive and often rationed so fires were lit with whatever scraps could be found. Paper, wood, even old shoes. Children would huddle in beds under coats or old sacks passed down generations and patched up beyond recognition.

School, for some, was both a lifeline and a source of dread. At least they were inside and mostly warm, but discipline was strict, and teachers had little time to nurture. The belt was used freely and it was just another place to be shouted at by an adult. Teachers had no time for softness. Children would be taught the basics, the three 'R's' – reading, writing and arithmetic.

And while education would offer a sliver of hope for some, for most, it was something to endure until they reached the age of 14 and could leave to start work, usually in the markets, in service cleaning, or hauling coal around the streets.

Playtime was outside, against a backdrop of rats, disease, and the smog from the factories. Illness was an accepted fact of life. Tuberculosis, diphtheria, and rickets were rife. Many families lost more than one child before they could reach adulthood. Medical care came in the form of home remedies, borrowed advice from neighbours which was usually 'old wives tales', or quite simply hoping for the best. It was just life.

But where there was hardship, there was also resilience. Children grew up quick-witted and tough. Because they had to be. Neighbours looked after neighbours, and families, however fractured, held on tightly to what they had. Poverty shaped them but it didn't define them.

Mary Ann Murphy was one of those children.

Poverty didn't matter to her, for Mary Ann it was affection. She was starved of tenderness, of care, of love. She longed for it. She felt abandoned and alone. Just like Cinderella, young Mary dreamed of a new life with a loving family.

She yearned for someone to love and love her back. When she cried for her mother, she was rewarded with a beating and told to "get on with it, she's dead, she's never coming back."

Perhaps her terrible start in life dictated the choices she would go on to make as an adult. The abandonment and coldness she experienced led her to fear rejection and loss. It may help explain why she struggled to nurture relationships, with partners, with her children.

Children learn from experience. And all she knew was people flitting in and out, rage, violence, and fear.

But I'd be doing her an injustice if I left it there, because my mother was not an angry child. In fact, she was very much the opposite. Everyone who knew her said she was a 'happy little thing', a 'joy', 'a good laugh', 'exciting to be with'.

School for Mary was exciting. It was a place where she could learn, be creative, and exist without the constant fear of a beating or being screamed at.

One of my mother's cousins, who now lives abroad, told me recently that Mary was actually a very intelligent child who excelled at school. So much so, she was awarded a scholarship to Notre Dame High School in Glasgow. At the time, it was one of the most prestigious girls' schools in the country, mostly attended by the daughters of wealthy families, and out of reach for most children growing up in poverty.

Notre Dame is now a state-funded secondary school, but back then, it was a fee-paying institution. Mary's teacher recognised her ability and identified her as a candidate for the entry exam, which allowed bright working-class girls to attend. She passed. But she never went. Nobody knows why and Mary never spoke of it but it seems a shame she was denied this life-changing opportunity.

When I try to piece together my mum's life, I only

know little bits and pieces. Learning about her scholarship reminded me that it was just one more thing I didn't know about her. One more part of her story that was never shared. It hammers home the reality that although she gave birth to me, I didn't know her at all.

It makes me wish I had been able to get to know her properly. If only we had the benefit of hindsight. But it's hardly surprising that I know so little. You see, my mother abandoned me when I was two. She just got up and walked out of the family home and never looked back.

I'd love to be able to tell you more about Mary Ann Murphy as a child. But there isn't anyone left alive who can tell me.

I'm not looking for the drama or the sensational details but for the ordinary things that make up a life. A favourite song. An everyday memory shared in passing.

I used to ask questions of those who knew her, those who remembered her. Most had only little fragments to offer. Her funny wee laugh or cackle as some described it. A phrase she would say. A smile she gave at a wedding or a story told in the pub. Nobody had the full picture. But every scrap has mattered to me.

On the surface, according to those who knew her and my vague memories, Mary appeared to be a fun-loving character who lived life to the full. I believe this was an act to satisfy her public. She was an attractive woman, but it was her charming, bubbly personality that drew people to her like moths to a flame. She had vibrant red hair, big beautiful blue eyes and an expressive smile.

Some people called her 'Ginger Murphy' – a nickname she quite liked. She thought it sounded very 'Hollywood'. What she lacked in height – she was five foot tall in her bare feet – she more than made up for in personality. Ginger Murphy wasn't classically beautiful but her *joie de vivre* was intoxicating to men and women alike. Whenever she went to Maggie McGhee's tea dances, the women loved to listen to her 'Glesgae' patter with funny stories and gossip.

Maggie was a local woman who had set up a get-together group in St Simon's Church hall for women only. Known affectionately as the 'auld hens', it was somewhere they could meet, dance, have a cup of tea and escape their mundane routines of being tied to the kitchen sink.

Mum loved to sing 'Nobody's Child' – perhaps it was how she felt about herself. She actually said she preferred The Alexander Brothers' version because they were her cousins. The Alexander Brothers were a very famous Scottish singing duet from 1950 until around 2012.

Over the years I have trawled public records, looked through old newspaper clippings and library archives. I searched for her in old electoral rolls, in baptism registers, anywhere I could think of on the internet that might hold some information. There was nothing to be found.

I had to rely on my imagination as there are no known photographs of Mum as a child. Sometimes, I imagined her on a doorstep as a girl looking up at the sky dreaming of a better life. Other times I imagined nothing at all because there was simply not enough to go on.

What I have discovered is that the past is slippery. The truth doesn't sit still. It changes shape depending on who's telling it, or what they remember, or what they'd rather forget. People protect the dead in ways they don't protect the living.

I've had moments where I felt close to her – closer than we were in life. Hearing someone's voice catch when they spoke about her. Finding out she once loved to dance. Or that she loved to sing. And there were moments when I felt the loss all over again, not just of her, but of the mother I never got to know. She gave birth to me but I didn't really know her.

This journey hasn't given me all the answers and I don't think it ever could. But it has given me something else – an understanding. A way I can hold the pain and the love. To see Mary Ann Murphy not just as a woman who left her children and died a horrible death, but as a young girl who was left behind.

As someone shaped by a city, a time, and a grief that was never spoken aloud.

It seems rather sad that my mum's name is recognised in Scotland, not for crowning achievements or glory, but because she died in an awful violent way.

Whenever I think of her life, the more I learn or uncover, the more I am consumed by the thought that the cold violent start to her young life seemed like an omen for what was to come at the end.

Mary and her aunts lived in Walker Street, Partick. It was the street she had lived in all her life and it's where I was born too.

It wasn't unusual for families to all live in the same street if not the same house. Generations of families would grow up together and you would have this huge support network – mostly babysitters if you needed them. It wasn't uncommon for food to be shared around as well.

Partick is an area of Glasgow on the north side of the river and just across from Govan.

Before it was annexed by the city in 1912, it was a separate burgh from Glasgow.

To this day it still has its own people and culture and is probably one of more famous areas in the city when people speak about Glasgow. This is probably mostly due to its most famous former resident – Sir Billy Connolly.

Billy lived with his family in White Street before moving to Stewartville Street. It's not uncommon to find older people recalling their own stories of when the comedy legend was a youngster. Everyone has a Connolly story. Whether they are true or not is neither here nor there because he is so well-loved by Glaswegians that just telling a story about him is deemed as entertainment and makes people feel important.

Generations of Partickonians still live, work and die in the area. Until fairly recently it was a hive of industry which started as a centre for the milling industry. Dominating the Glasgow skyline for years was the massive but iconic Meadowside Granary. You couldn't miss it at 13 storeys high with huge gantries that we, as children, thought were giant slides.

It estimated that over five million bricks were used in its construction which was a lot for its time and probably generated a lot of work in the area.

In 1960 they added an extension which doubled the holding space of Meadowside and made it the largest grain store in Europe. This was important because the Clyde was still a booming port back then. It closed in 1998 and was finally demolished in 2002, but not before it featured in a cult Scottish film called *Small Faces* in 1996.

The area is now called Glasgow Harbour Project and features highrise housing and a riverside walkway. The impressive Riverside Museum (the Museum of Transport) is also located there.

The area has changed dramatically from my mother's time, indeed mine too. I often feel pangs of sadness when I see another change, especially when it's student flats or bland housing estates.

Old style buildings might have been ugly, but one thing they did have was character – much like the souls who lived and worked in them.

A lot of those new builds may not be on sites of importance for historians, but there are memories on every corner or building for people like myself and my mother's generation.

Where there used to stand someone's home now stands a bar. The streets I would play in with my sister no longer exist either. In my day there were hardly any cars around and the streets were safer for children to play. I look at the modern flash cars and remember simpler times with a smile and a hankering for the horse and carts that still trotted around the streets when I was a child.

The cart was mostly used by the rag and bone man who would take your unused clothes or knick knacks for a few pennies. At the very least, the child trying to give him their stuff would leave with a balloon. The women were cannier. They did most of the bartering with the rag man.

Another memory comes to the fore: the 'hudgie' on the back of a coal lorry. It was a common sight to see young people huddled together on the back of the lorry for a wee hurl along the road. Many a time you would fall off and skin your knees, but the biggest injury was usually to your pride when you got caught and would get a slap to the back of your head in front of your pals.

Back then, everyone lived in the famous Glasgow tenements – stone buildings built during the industrial revolution to accommodate a growing population. Most of these have been knocked down and rebuilt to suit a more modern style.

The tenements were often three or four storeys high and on each level there could be three houses with as many as eight or more occupants. Some were called single ends with one room or, if you were really lucky and could afford it, a room and a kitchen. When I say kitchen, it was more an area within the room for cooking and washing up. Families would live, eat and sleep in that single room. There were no toilets or bathing facilities. There would be one outside toilet for each level in the building.

You have not known cold until you're standing in the dead of night waiting to be able to use the toilet dressed in just your nightgown. We didn't have the luxury of heated throws or dressing gowns.

I remember wearing jumpers to bed because it was so cold. If you were lucky enough to have a blanket it was usually thin and rough – scratchy we used to say. There wasn't such a thing as fabric softener in my childhood.

If you wanted a proper bath instead of a wash at the sink then it was off to Douglas Street (now Purdon Street) to use the public baths. Opened in 1914, it was known as 'the steamie' where local women would do their washing. Years later, in 1987, actor and playwright, Tony Roper, would write an award-winning play based on a 'steamie' set in 1950 which is still shown to audiences today.

It was a common sight to see women walking along the street with their weans in a pram, dirty laundry tied up in a sheet or in a tin bath filled to the brim. The laundry would be done by hand and was extremely hard work; the women would use this tedious chore as an excuse to meet up with their friends and gather local gossip.

While it was used by women for washing and chewing the fat (Scots speak for conversation), men typically used it for more practical reasons – bathing. A bath was a luxury many could ill-afford so unless you were feeling flush, this consisted of a wash at the kitchen sink or a tin bath dragged into the middle of the room and filled with water boiled in pots.

The luxury of a long hot bath was not for us. Oh no, your dad would use it first, then maybe mum and then the oldest child down to the youngest. You can imagine the colour of the water by the time it reached the youngest. If you had grandparents living with you, as was common, it was an even longer wait and dirtier water. It's not surprising that there were constant outbreaks of dysentery, scabies, gastroenteritis, chickenpox and measles as well as infestations of rats.

But that was life, and people didn't know any better. You made it what you could.

2
—

Love and Marriage

MARY LOVED living in Walker Street. She had lots of friends but mostly hung around with a group of boys. She preferred their rough and tumble games to playing 'houses' with the girls. As she grew older, her interest in the boys changed from just being friends to wanting more. The object of her affections was John Cullen who lived a few streets away from Mary in Dunaskin Street.

John and Mary were part of the same gang who would roam the streets from morning until night. In those days, children went home when the street lights came on at night. The children made their own entertainment and mostly gathered at a local park or swing park as we call them. Everyone in the neighbourhood would congregate there.

Mary and John had developed a close bond and

when they became teenagers, romance blossomed. I remember my mother telling me years later she was besotted by John and wanted him to feel the same way. She thought he was the most handsome boy on the planet.

'I know the feeling,' I wanted to say, but didn't. She might not have brought me up, but she was still my mother. I couldn't be unkind to her, but I wanted to take her by the shoulders and scream: 'What about wanting to be besotted by your children, of loving and being loved by us? Why wasn't that enough?' But of course, I didn't.

I wish I had. Sometimes when I let myself think about those last few times I saw her, I wonder if having difficult and frank conversations might have changed her future and ours? It's probably a very childish way of looking at it because fate is fate isn't it? No matter what you do.

To teenage Mary, John was the escape she needed from her nasty aunts and mean cousins. But her father was troubled when he found out his impressionable daughter wanted to take up with John. As far as George Murphy was concerned, John Cullen was a thug who would bring nothing but misery to his daughter. John had 'street cred' and had been in more than a few scraps or fights.

This didn't worry Mary, in fact it excited her. John suited her personality and with him around to protect her, she felt nobody would ever be able to take advantage of her again. She was quick to let the other girls in their gang know she was his girlfriend in case any of them had ideas that John would be theirs.

Mary dreamed of marrying John and having their own home. It was her only ambition.

But there was a fly in the ointment – John's friend Richie. The two boys were inseparable, and this rankled with Mary and riled her up to an unreasonable fury. She instantly disliked him and vice versa. She felt jealous of the way John appeared to idolise Richie. Whenever the boys wanted to hang with each other, Mary was dropped like hot coal. It stung and she resented the young lad badly.

Years later she told me a story about him which was disturbing, despite her telling it in her usual sing-song cheery voice. Mum had been desperate to go to a dance in Maggie McGees at Partick Cross. John had promised he would take her but he canceled on the night saying Richie needed his help with something. This conversation sticks in my head not least because she uses a term we would consider derogatory today.

"You promised me, John," she cried.

"I know, Mary, but something has come up."

"What's so important he needs you?"

"I don't know, he will tell me when he sees me, Mary."

"What are you, a pair of p**fs?"

John raised an eyebrow but ignored her comment. She wasn't winding him up, not today.

"Mary, you know the score, Richie has helped me out many a time. We've been pals since primary school."

"Oh, so he says jump and you ask how high? Well, I'm no playing second fiddle to him every time. If you cannae tell him you're no going then I will!"

John told her the job would only take a few hours and he'd meet her after the dance. He began to walk away and Mary let rip.

"If I see that big Nancy boy I'll be telling him a thing or two. You can let me down but not him, ya arselicker ye."

As she was walking away in a temper Richie appeared in front of her coming from another direction.

"Oi, you! Big man! I want a word with you."

She wanted to know why he needed John on their date night. Richie told her to mind her own business and she physically lashed out at him. She didn't imagine he would hit her back. In those days, if there was an issue with a man's significant other, they would ask the man to deal with it before they got a smack.

Richie maintained he didn't intend to hit Mary, but when he saw her hand coming towards his face, he instinctively got the first punch in.

It burst her nose open. She refused to go to the hospital for treatment and it left a small dent in the bridge of her nose. She told people it was from a diseased bone she had in childhood. She told her father she walked into a door. Mary never did get to the dance that night and in future she steered clear of Richie as much as possible.

Mum was determined nothing was getting in the way of her relationship with John. Until he was called up to the war in 1944 as soon as he turned 18. Mary was devastated and begged John not to go. She didn't understand that the young man didn't have a choice. He wanted to go and fight for his country. He spent many hours consoling Mary and reassuring her that he would still want her when he returned.

Mary begged and pleaded with John to marry her before he left but he refused. He didn't know how long he would be gone or if he would even come back at all. Everyone knew thousands of young soldiers were dying every day during the Second World War. There were very few families immune to the horrors the war drove home.

John told Mary they were too young to marry and she just needed to wait for him to return. She countered if he loved her, he'd marry her. She told him she wouldn't wait, she'd go off and find someone else. Mary thought her ultimatum would work – it didn't. He felt Mary was being overdramatic and emotional and was confident she would be waiting when he came back.

Mary was heartbroken. She'd been abandoned once again.

Joe Mullen was born in Stirlingshire but his family moved to Albion Street in Glasgow when he was a young boy. Later in his life they moved to Hollybrook Street in Govanhill.

Joe was a kind man who was hardworking and gentle in nature. He was close to his mother and would often seek her counsel when things were troubling him.

I'm unsure how Mary and Joe met. It wasn't something I thought to ask either of them but I wish I'd been more 'nosy' as a child. There has been some talk that they met at a tea dance during the war and other people said he was part of the same gang she was in.

What I do know is they met soon after John left and Joe was happy to supply the attention Mary was craving. She lapped it up. Joe and Mary married in November 1945 and just nine months later my oldest brother John was born. I remember Mum telling me she was the big topic of conversation for a while after that. She said it with her usual chuckle and shrug of her shoulders. She didn't care what people thought of her.

Mum told me at first she was very happy with Joe. He was a good man and she felt loved and protected for the first time in her life. She knew he would never leave her or cheat on her.

Marriage to Joe wasn't enough for her. As far as she was concerned he was a weak man, despite clinging to him like you would a life raft in the ocean. She came to despise his affable gentle manner and his liking for a pint after a hard day's work, leaving her to feed and organise their brood most nights.

He was the rebound man, the man she sought out to help ease her heartbreak over John. It's all too easy to say now she should've just dated Joe until their relationship ran its natural course instead of rushing headlong into marriage. If only we all had the benefit of hindsight.

Joe's shortcomings and feebleness bored her. She found his habit of running to his mother with every problem annoying. Mary needed strength, guidance and passion. Things that were lacking in Joe Mullen. Over the course of a few years, Mary and Joe had five more children together. After John was born, came Kathleen, Margaret, Carol, me then Marie, the youngest, in 1956. Soon after, the cracks in their relationship began to show.

Mary saw life as a Glasgow housewife 'dreary'. She felt like she was missing out on excitement and attention. Wiping children's noses was boring and she felt her life was one of drudgery. She didn't want to stay at home to look after her children and make sure her husband's food was on the table for him coming back from work. She had an aversion to Joe 'ruling the roost' and doing as she was told. Nowadays, in this supposed enlightened world, we would call it coercive controlling behaviour.

Perhaps it threw up unwanted memories of her 'Cinderella' years where as a child she was chief cook, cleaner and bottle washer. I want to be sympathetic to my mother and say her early years and the trauma she suffered skewered her judgement as she got older. I don't want to think unkind thoughts that perhaps she just didn't want to be a mother. I have always believed she was lost with no-one to understand or support her.

Instead of feeling angry with her, I feel sad for her. Despite her intelligence, her emotional needs wiped out any common sense and she found herself in situations she didn't want to be in. For instance, looking after her own children.

When I was two, my mother walked out of her marriage, her home and us, her children. Marie was just a baby. Years later, Kathleen, my eldest sister, told me the story of the straw that broke the camel's back.

It was a freezing cold January night and Dad hadn't come home from work with his wages. Mum told her to fetch John, our brother, as she would need to go and get Dad out the pub otherwise he would spend all his wages and there would be no food.

Kathleen didn't have a scarf or gloves and the thick smog made it difficult to see but she heard the voices of youths ahead of her.

John jumped out from behind her, giving her a fright. Instinctively, she slapped him.

"You deserved that slap. We need to go, Ma wants us to go to Govanhill with her."

"Why?"

"Da hasn't come in again with his pay. If she doesn't get to the pub we won't have any food."

Kathleen said by the time they got back to the house, Margaret was dressed and Carol, who was only four weeks old, was in the pram.

She told Kathleen to tell the bus driver she was under five so she could get on the bus for free. She only had enough money for her and John's fare.

Mum intended to leave the kids at their Gran's house until she could get Dad out of the pub. The pub was closing at 10pm and time was not on Mum's side. If she didn't get there before closing, Dad would disappear until his money was gone.

Gran was not the kindest and was bedridden with ill-health. She wasn't happy when Mum turned up with four hungry children in tow. Kathleen said the only bonus was her Gran always had bread and jam so that's what we had for dinner that night.

When Mary got to the pub, she was manhandled by the barman who said no women were allowed in. She was furious and said she wasn't leaving until Dad gave her money for her 'starving weans'.

She wasted no time in verbally laying into Joe before pouring a pint of lager over him. Joe's dad tried to intervene and asked what kind of woman came into a man's pub?

"And what kind of man leaves his weans hungry while he drinks and gambles?"

The barman again tried to forcibly remove her but Mum stood fast.

"What do you know, you fat baldy bastard? What if it was your weans without any food?"

Someone called the police to eject her from the premises.

Mum was defiant and did not leave quietly. On her way out she lifted what glasses she could and hurled them at the gantry.

She was taken to the police station and charged with assault and breach of the peace. Because of the children, she was allowed out on bail but at 2am, Dad refused to let Mum take them out of the house. She was sent away without any money and forced to walk the three miles back to our house.

Dad kept the children at his mum's until the following Sunday. When they arrived home, they saw Mum hadn't been there. She had disappeared and as a child I was told she went to be with her true love, John. When my grandfather, Mary's father, heard this he was furious and swore he'd give Mary the "beating of her life". He'd never liked John and had a grudging respect for Joe. Mum steered away from her own father for a long time afterwards because she knew he'd keep his promise.

Of course she eventually went back to Joe because myself and Marie were born soon after this. Kathleen said they would have some terrible rows during this time which usually resulted in one of them storming out.

As their marriage continued to break down, Mum and Dad grew further and further apart until one day, when Marie was just a baby, and I was two years old, she left and this time she never came back.

My mother thought the grass would be greener with John, who had returned from war, and that he would bring passion and excitement instead of poverty and dirty nappies. Maybe it was like that at first – free from the shackles of a husband and six children – but before long trouble was brewing again.

Their relationship was volatile. When she told John she was pregnant with child number seven and his first, he wasn't ready. He liked the freedom of single life and enjoyed going to the pub with his friends. And, if truth be told, he wasn't ready for a commitment to Mary – it was nine months since she had left Joe and John questioned whether he was indeed the father to the child.

They began to fight a lot, so much so the neighbours could hear every word. Mary gave as good as she got verbally from John and although she was no match for him physically, she still stood up to him during their arguments. At times she would pick up the nearest object and throw it at him.

Their fights would sometimes escalate to such an extent the neighbours would step in and separate them for their own safety. Very rarely did police get called – domestic violence wasn't something they intervened with in those days.

Mary was beginning to realise the grass wasn't greener with John and he was no hero. But, despite it all, she loved him, and they had four more children together after Michael, their first, was born. Martin, Patricia and twins Brian and David.

Once, in a fit of temper after another fight, Mary registered Michael as a Mullen – and named Joe as his father.

Although parental DNA testing was first used in the 1920s, it was expensive and out of reach to working class people, so John accepted that Michael was his son, and he was known as a Cullen all through his life, despite what the register said.

John worked hard to provide for his family. He was away a lot as a lorry driver working long hours which gave respite from his troubled relationship with Mary. Her children from both men could bring Mary no peace, no joy, no comfort. Sometimes she would flit in and out of our lives and we would have our mother back for a brief period. Who she mothered was dependent on which man she was with at the time. When Joe was in favour, my mum was back in our lives. But when they inevitably fought and she left him for John, we were motherless again. I was so young I don't even remember those instances.

Today, Mary would probably have been diagnosed with Post Traumatic Stress Disorder as a result of a bereaved and abusive childhood. But back in the 60s and 70s, she was seen as a homewrecker, a lush, a woman who deserted her children. There was no sympathy, no understanding of why Mary couldn't settle down or find the happiness she so desperately needed.

She was closest to Kathleen and Carol who were the oldest. They often went to parties together where she would tell the girls to say she was their sister. Meanwhile, Margaret had told people from a young age her mother was dead.

Whatever the reasons for mum's behaviour, there is no denying it has had a profound effect on all of our lives.

Her relationship with John collapsed. She had gone from the frying pan into the fire. When she'd been with my dad, she would run to John with her troubles and he would comfort her. In Mary's eyes, John was her 'knight in shining armour'. It didn't take long for that illusion to be shattered.

In 1971 they split up and Mary sought refuge in alcohol. There was solace in the bottom of a glass.

3

A Glasgow Childhood

WHEN I came along in 1954, I was Joe Mullen and Mary's fifth child. She had already left Joe once not long before I was born, and she would leave again soon after I took my first steps.

My parents' marriage was difficult and troubled and I'm quite sure that if given the chance Mary would've taken contraception long before I was conceived. But Mum and Dad were from staunch Catholic families who believed that birth control should be natural and interfering in it was meddling with God's will.

Childhood for myself and my siblings was not easy. Money was hard to come by and people did what they could to get along. Poverty was rife in Scotland because of high unemployment rates, declining industries and desperately poor housing conditions.

I suppose you could say on paper we were luckier than

most as Dad worked. But he was a single father with six children so his wages, such as they were, didn't stretch very far at all. Money was in short supply.

My oldest sister, Kathleen, their secondborn child, was a designated babysitter, but she was still a child herself so sometimes we would be sent to our great-aunts' house. Kathleen made sure we got up in time for school, dressed us all and made sure we helped her to clean the house. It can't have been easy for her at all.

I was a 'daddy's girl'. I adored him. He was a gentle, placid man who never once raised his voice to me and only occasionally do I remember hearing a cross word to my older brother and sisters.

I remember feeling sad that my mum didn't love him as much as I did. He was a good man who didn't beat her, didn't cheat on her and tried his best to provide for his family. But perhaps that was his problem, he was just a normal man in those days and this wasn't enough for Mary.

I never saw him with another woman after Mum left but sometimes he would say he'd missed the bus home from the pub and had to stay with a friend overnight. I wonder now if this is when he indulged in romantic liaisons. It's a shame he never found anyone to settle down with because he had so much love to give to the right woman.

His only failing and one which I disliked intensely was

every Saturday he would leave the house and be in the pub from 10am until 11pm. I hated it because my older siblings fought like cats and dogs and would have some ferocious fights. To this day, I cannot bear raised voices and will run from confrontation and arguments. They would often go out themselves and leave myself and Marie, my baby sister, to fend for ourselves.

In the summer months, our neighbour, Mrs McCandlish, would spot Marie and I sitting in the close and would feel sorry for us and invite us over to her house. Some of the other neighbours would also take us in.

We were too scared to stay in our own house because everyone knew our door was left unlocked and strangers would often just wander in. Usually other teenagers but to Marie and I it was terrifying.

Dad, of course, was oblivious to all this and thought we were being looked after by our brother and sisters but then one of the neighbours told him what was happening. He was aghast and for a while he stopped going out but then his shame would be forgotten and the lure of a pint and the pub was too much and the cycle would begin again.

As I've said before, money was short. There was never enough to go round and it wasn't unusual for us to be sent to bed early to try and beat the hunger pangs. In the 50s, the welfare system was virtually non-existent. There was no such thing as help from the state. Families would help each other as much as they could but everyone was skint and there wasn't a lot to go around. Dinner quite often consisted of three slices of bread between five of us with margarine or sugar spread thinly on top. We would get half a slice each and wash it down with water. Dad wouldn't let us drink until we had finished the food such as it was.

I remember when I learned to read and picked books from the library or school, Enid Blyton's Famous Five books always had fantastic descriptions of the delicious food the children were eating such as ham, bacon, eggs, jam sandwiches, cakes and lashings of ginger beer. I was jealous of these fictional children and their fantastic lifestyles and wondered how they had so much money when we had nothing. I remember Kathleen telling me not to read such rubbish and that it was just fantasy.

I lost myself in books whenever I could and devoured the pages and especially loved stories where the children had a loving, kind mother. I missed having a mother so much. I loved my dad and he did the best he could, but every child needs a mother. I longed for mine. I wanted cuddles, I wanted someone to read me bedtime stories and tuck me in and look after me when I was sick. Dad did his best but he wasn't Mum and he didn't have a woman's instinct for looking after children.

They say children learn from their mothers and so far the only thing the Mullen children had learnt from her was abandonment and misery. My dad once told me that my Mum's only downfall was that she was a beautiful woman. I did not grasp what he meant. He did say he loved her, but she never loved him back. Her absence was felt in virtually every aspect of my young life, especially at school which was horrendous for me.

It wasn't a secret she had left us and children can be so cruel taunting you for not having a mum.

In some ways it might have been easier if she'd died, but everyone knew she didn't want us and had just scarpered. It was humiliating.

John, Kathleen, Margaret and Carol learned how to survive if they got picked on but Marie and I were quite sensitive children. We became easy targets for the bullies. I wouldn't fight back and would just retreat into a corner and cry. Almost daily I would find myself hiding to avoid another beating or taunting. Sometimes, if they were in a benevolent mood, my older siblings would chase the bullies away.

When I was around six years old, a horrible thing happened to me. In the aftermath, I began crying myself to sleep and soiling the bed. I could not bear to tell my dad why and no matter how much he tried, he could not console me. Sex and sexual matters were taboo in Dad's house. It was completely forbidden so how could I tell my dad that one of his friends had been abusing me?

It happened during the summer holidays when Dad had gone to work. Kathleen was babysitting as usual. I remember it was a boiling hot day; summers in Scotland were quite often stifling hot.

My dad's friend, who we shall call Walter, had come to decorate the living room. I had been outside playing at skipping with my siblings when I went in for the toilet and to get a drink of water.

Walter asked who was with me and when I said no-one he asked me to help him with the wallpaper. He asked what size shoe I was and said he would check. I had my back to him and instead of lifting my shoes, he pulled down my pants. Fear gripped me. This didn't feel right I thought and began to cry.

A second later the door was knocked and Walter quickly jumped back.

"Don't tell anyone about this, I'll get you sweeties. It's our secret."

I ran from the room as fast as my little legs would carry me.

I never told anyone about that incident and I never told my dad why I was crying every day for months afterwards.

I made sure I was never left alone with Walter ever again and when I was older I did wonder if having my mother around would've protected me from such incidents?

As I grew up, puberty was especially difficult. When I got my first period, I had no idea what was happening to me, but my dad gently explained to me what was going on. It can't have been easy for him, men did not usually get involved in 'women's problems' but he handled it as subtly as he could. I didn't know then that it would be my first and only lesson in sex education from my father.

He said, "I know you have blood, so you are a woman now. You need to be careful with boys, don't let any of them near you, they will tell you all sorts of things to get to go near you and touch you where they shouldn't, and try to get you to have sex. They can say they love you when they don't. I know, I was a boy once myself. You must save yourself until marriage."

And that was it.

Sex education lesson over.

He had done what he regarded as his duty. I just remember the shame and embarrassment I felt hearing him speak the words and wished my mother was there. I can actually laugh now when I think about how he must have been feeling the same way. Poor Dad.

Despite his limitations in handling little girls, dad and I had a good relationship. I was a clingy child who followed him everywhere and did things just to try and please him. At times he would put the fear of God into me making sure I behaved. He would tell us that God sees everything and if we misbehave we would go to hell and into the bad fire. It terrified the life out of me. I now realise it was the only way he knew how to keep six children in check.

Life can't have been easy for him either. He was an anomaly – a man raising his own children without a woman was virtually unheard off. He took his role seriously and while it may seem like we were being dragged up, we didn't know any different. I'm sure a lot of what happened to us as youngsters would be seen as some form of child abuse now but back then it was just the way it was.

With money always being tight, there were times when we just couldn't go to school because we had no shoes and there was no money to buy any. When you didn't turn up for class, the teacher would report your non-attendance to the school board who would then send out a truant officer (skiving inspector as we called them) to your house to check why you were absent. You had to have a good reason for being off school and woe betide any child caught skipping school just to have a day off. Not only would you get a belt from the teacher but you'd also get a smack at home although in our house, dad left the smacking to the teachers.

If you were absent from school because you didn't have any school uniform, dad would be issued with a slip of paper to attend the welfare office in John Street.

This was a revolving door for my family because there was always one of us who needed something and as hard as dad worked, there just wasn't enough money to go around. Getting any part of your uniform from the welfare office was a humiliation all in itself.

The shoes, jackets and other uniform pieces they handed out were standard regulation items given out to the poor and needy. They were instantly recognisable as "poor people shoes" and you'd be looked down on by everyone, even the teachers, for wearing them.

To this day, I still remember the feelings of shame and embarrassment having to wear these garments. It's only now as an adult that I think about the lack of food and basic clothing while Dad always managed to have enough money for all day drinking sessions in the pub.

4

Wee Joe in The Drum

WE WERE a Catholic family and had to go to mass most weekends. When I was seven, it was time for me to take my first Holy Communion. This is a Catholic rite of passage when children are considered mature enough to go from being a 'child of God' to becoming a Christian.

Of course, I was too young to understand that and for me it was all about getting to wear a dress like a bride. I was so excited for it and for weeks beforehand I would ask my dad if it was the day yet. It was going to be so wonderful. I had a beautiful dress to wear. It was white cotton and had lace around it. My aunt Lottie, who was in charge of the day, also managed to get me a little hairband to wear which had a veil attached to it. Best of all, I had new shoes – not hand-me-downs like everything else or from the welfare. They were white flat plimsole style. I felt so pretty.

It was considered a huge occasion but I was sad when Dad told me he wouldn't be able to come and I'd have to go stay with Aunt Lottie the night before. "Mum most definitely wouldn't be there," he said. It took some of the shine off the day for me.

But Aunt Lottie told me I'd get lots of pennies especially if we timed a walk along the street right for the men going in and out of the pubs. It was tradition – most Catholic adults would stop and hand you coins for your little purse. Except I didn't have a purse or bag, I had an old bloody black shoe polish tin and the coins would slide about and you could hear me rattling before you saw me. On the upside, by the end of the day the tin was full and no more rattling. I do remember my tin being taken from me. Dad probably needed it for food or something. I remember him saying it was about 12.5p in total and I was allowed to take back a few sixpenny pieces to get myself some sweets.

Aunt Lottie took me to the Venetian Cafe near Partick Cross for tea afterwards. This was a proper treat and even Aunt Lottie devouring a whole plate of food like Desperate Dan didn't sour my delight at the cakes and sandwiches I was treated to that day. It was only later I felt sad that everyone else had their mums all dressed in their finery and I didn't.

Our family home screamed poverty. When I say home it was just one room. It had belonged to my maternal grandfather, who my mum named me after. George Murphy had died long before I was born. When I was around three years old, Dad received a letter to say the tenements in Walker Street were to be demolished. He wasn't very happy about this as the house held lots of memories for him but he understood that a move would be good for us.

A new council estate was being built on the outskirts of Bearsden and Drumchapel and a lot of families from Partick were invited to apply for a new house. We were successful and dad was allocated a house in Drumchapel which locals dubbed 'The Drum'. While the house did not fully meet the needs of our large family, compared to what we had been living in it was sheer luxury. It was a modern tenement which was only three storeys high and would house five other families with two on each level.

Our flat was a three bedroom but it also had an indoor bathroom, a living room and a kitchen and was one of the larger homes. It was sparsely furnished with linoleum on the floors but Dad added what he could in terms of furniture. The only source of heating, a coal fire, was in the living room. We did have electric lights and a gas cooker, and they were operated by coins.

Dad had to make sure there was a supply of shillings (a shilling is equal to 5p in today's money) in case the meter ran out. When we didn't have any money for it, food would be cooked on top of the coal fire. In the summer, running out of meter money didn't seem so bad as it didn't get dark until bedtime and we could tolerate cold food due to the heat outside.

Winter was a very different story. The house would be plunged into darkness, and we would use candles for light. No-one wanted the job of going to the coal bunker to fill a bucket with coal. We all had to take a turn doing that. Because there were so many of us, we would lose track of whose turn it was.

Huddled together for warmth, we would vote who was going. I was particularly terrified of this as one of my great-aunts used to lock me in their cupboard, so I developed a fear of small dark places. My brother and sisters would promise they would not scare whoever had to go but you can be sure their word would quickly be broken.

My brother would often hide in the bunker and jump out when the door was opened. The others would make eerie noises and shout about ghosts in the house when it was pitch black. Because the doors would creak it was quite scary especially to this four-year-old.

On the days we would have four slices of toasted bread for breakfast, lunch, dinner and supper, I would go to bed hungry and dream of the day when I would have my own house. I thought how wonderful it would be to choose a husband with a good job, have children, have nice clothes and nice furniture. And to never go hungry again. It lit a fire in my belly and kept me warm inside during dark days.

Dad was a plumber's mate and worked in John Brown's Shipyard in Clydebank. A major employer in the area, they built many famous ships including the Queen Elizabeth II and HMS Hood. Nicknamed 'the mighty hood', it was the largest warship in the world for over 20 years. At Brown's height, from the 1900s to the 1950s, it was not only the most famous but also one of the most highly regarded shipbuilding companies in the world.

Dad probably thought his job was secure for life but before the unions became a thing, Browns made thousands of workers redundant and he was one of them. There were heavy repercussions from this. A major one being he couldn't keep up with the rent payments for the house.

By this time, my brother had gone down to England to work where he met a girl and married her. He decided to make England his home. One of my older sisters was married, another was due to get married, one was living independently and that left myself and my baby sister at home with Dad.

I was 14 when we were evicted. When the eviction notice was served, he found a neighbour willing to look after my little sister, Marie. He was going to live with his brother and wife. They had 14 children of their own so there was no room for me.

It would be years before I would look back and wonder how my dad could've left me at such a young age to find my own way. I had no choice but to go seek out my mum and ask if I could live with her.

My mother was living in a top floor tenement in the Maryhill area of Glasgow with John and their five children. It had two rooms, a living room and a kitchen. I was living there for about three weeks when Mum walked out and disappeared. John, not being unkind I must say, did not feel it was appropriate for me to stay there without Mum. He told me I would have to leave. I had nowhere to go. I was lost.

Carol, my older sister, was staying with her future in-laws. She had an empty flat with no electricity or hot water. There was no furniture or bedding and it had an outside toilet. She planned to move in after her wedding. I remember walking the four miles to see her after John threw me out. I haven't forgotten her kindness in letting me stay in her flat. It was a better option than a freezing stairwell.

I went back to Mum's — ironically just one street away from Carol's flat — to see if she had returned. She hadn't.

John asked where I was staying and when I told him I was sleeping in my sister's empty flat he gave me some bedding and an old fur coat, presumably Mum's, and said he was so sorry for the way things had turned out and that he couldn't help me anymore. I was just grateful to have warm things to sleep with at night and I knew I was safe inside and not on the streets alone.

One morning I woke up covered in big red lumps all over my body. It seemed that either fleas or moths had taken a liking to the coat, and it was infested. They obviously preferred my warm blood and enjoyed a feast – which was a lot more than I was eating in those days. I spent the next few years going between my sister Carol's flat and living with friends. It was a tumultuous time of my life and I felt very unsettled. I was homeless, motherless and in desperate need of money.

I was nearly 16 when I found my first job as a cashier in Woolworths, which was in Argyle Street in the city centre. This meant I could actually rent my own room. I was so excited I went looking for Dad to tell him. I felt things were going to get better. I quite often spent Saturdays looking for dad in the pubs in Partick. Interestingly enough, Billy Connolly's dad, William, was one of my dad's drinking buddies. I quite often spoke with him when I was hunting Dad down.

Billy wasn't as famous at this point. He was just starting out his career with Gerry Rafferty in a duo they called The Humblebums. Of course, many years later when Billy revealed his dad had physically and sexually abused him as a child, I felt sad and shocked. William Connolly had seemed like a very amiable man who was proud of his son. My dad wouldn't have had a clue his friend was an abuser. It serves as a reminder to never judge because you never know what is going on in people's private lives.

Everyone knew my dad in Partick – he was known as 'Wee Joe'. On this particular day, I was sure I would find him in The Dolphin at Partick Cross, but no, he wasn't there. He would do his rounds between The Quarter Gill on Dumbarton Road, The Smiddy on Dumbarton Road, The Dowanhill on Dowanhill Street or The Three Judges at Partick Cross. He would often be in the bookies next to the Dolphin, but I kept missing him by minutes. I circled back to the first pub and sure enough he was in there.

As usual, he was smartly dressed in a three-piece suit, matching shirt and tie and his shoes shining. Dad prided himself on his clothes but more often than not his suit would go into the pawnbrokers on a Monday, and he would retrieve it on a Friday in time for his weekend drinking.

I remember it was a lovely and sunny day when I told him I was starting work at Woolworths – a huge retail chain known to everyone as 'Woolies'. It sold everything from clothes, books, toys and household goods. It was probably most famous for its Pick 'n' Mix range of sweeties. I was offered a position of cashier.

WEE JOE IN THE DRUM

I asked if he could help me out with bus fares and he said all he could spare was two shillings. He said he was sorry that was all he could give. He asked where I was staying, and I told him. I was so pleased with the job and my two shillings and, I guess, immaturity, to question why Dad could afford to gamble and drink but not give his daughter the basics in life.

5

First Job and First Love

IN THE summer of 1969, I started my job. I still did not know where my mum was but later found out through Kathleen that she was living close to the city centre.

One day I met one of my former neighbours from 'The Drum'. Celia Denny was a bus conductress and during our chat I mentioned my living situation and how dire it was. She offered me a room in her flat because she lived alone and did shift work. Celia said she lived in a flat in Kirkland Street which was close to the city centre which meant I could walk to work and save money on bus fares. It was also just five minutes from Mum's new flat in Vernon Street. Vernon Street doesn't actually exist now; it was pulled down and made into a continuation of Queen Margaret Drive.

FIRST JOB AND FIRST LOVE

This stroke of luck seemed too good to be true but it was. I will always be grateful to Celia for taking in a practically homeless teenage girl and giving her a roof over her head. My life seemed to change overnight.

I had money in my pocket, a warm clean home to live in and I was making new friends. For the first time in probably my whole life, I was happy. I loved my little job in Woolies too but I knew that I wasn't going to stay there forever. I finally felt free from stress and worry and could concentrate on making plans for my future. I had so many hopes and dreams.

My cousin Bridget came into my work one day. Even though I hadn't seen her for a few years, we recognised each other instantly. She was close in age to me so we had the same interests – namely music and dancing. Bridget asked if I wanted to go dancing with her and eagerly I agreed so we made plans.

I was nervous because I was underage but Bridget assured me nobody would ask. A little make up and some grown up clothes and I would get in, she said. Nobody questions it if you look old enough. There was no such thing as ID, who had passports then anyway?

I was 15 and felt invincible and excited. I had yet to discover boys and this felt like the perfect opportunity.

For our first night out we went to a club called Sergeant Peppers, named after The Beatles album, of course. It was in the Botanic Gardens at the top of Byers Road in the West End of Glasgow.

The venue actually used to be the Glasgow Corporation bus depot, but they closed it down and changed it into a dance hall.

I loved it at Sergeant Peppers and we lived for the weekends when we could go dancing. We were young, we were free and we loved to have a good time. It was my first night at Sergeant Peppers where I met the man who would become my husband.

At first it was his friend who kept asking me to dance and I didn't want to be rude so I said yes but I didn't fancy him. I made an excuse to go to the toilet and he said he would wait outside for me. I made Bridget stay with me in the loo while we waited for him to wander off but he didn't. We stayed in the toilet for what felt like an hour but was really only about 30 minutes. We thought he'd have gotten bored and left but he was still sitting outside the toilet waiting for me. I was mortified and ended up making an excuse to get away from him.

I had noticed a young man who I did fancy. He was handsome, tall and wearing a brown double breasted suit and pink shirt and brown brogue shoes. I thought he was the most beautiful man I'd ever seen.

He came over and asked me if I wanted to dance. Of course I said yes right away and then he used the classic chat up line: "Do you come here often?"

"Naw, its ma first time," I replied.

We danced for a little while then he said, "I need to go, I'm with someone. If you like we can meet again and go to another dance hall next week?"

I agreed right away and the next week we met at the Electric Gardens on Sauchiehall Street. That was the start of the romance. He swept me right off my feet. He was 19 and was just about to finish an apprenticeship as an electrician. Bridget used to joke that I was swooning over him and she wasn't wrong.

We spent a lot of time together once we were officially dating. We went to dancehalls all over Glasgow and on a Sunday morning I would drag myself out of bed to cheer him on from the sidelines while he played football.

My dad's warning was in the back of my mind and whenever my boyfriend and I were getting intimate, his words rang in my ears.

"Save yourself for marriage, Gina!"

But it wasn't enough to stop me. I loved him and I was enjoying the intimacy and the feelings of affection that came with your first flush of romance. I had no idea about the facts of life or contraception. With no female influence in my life such as my mother, it wasn't something anyone else in my life thought useful to tell me. My sweet-talking boyfriend convinced me I would not get pregnant and if I did he would marry me. How naïve was I?

'Patter-merchant' is a Scots phrase for someone who is charming, jokes a lot and has charisma. It's often used in line with 'could sell tea to China' and it's not meant as an insult. This was my boyfriend. A pure patter-merchant who coaxed and charmed his way into my bed.

There was no proposal of marriage, he just said, 'did I want to get engaged?'

We had been dating for nine months when in May 1970 I woke up being sick. I didn't think anything of it because we'd been out dancing the night before. I put it down to a hangover. But I kept vomiting and one morning it was so violent and noisy it woke my landlady who suggested I might be pregnant. She was divorced and a mother herself so she knew the signs. She advised me to go to the doctors for a test.

My doctor's surgery was in Maryhill at the top of Oran Street near Maryhill Road. I knew my mum was living in Vernon Street which was parallel with the street I was standing in. I was shell-shocked at the doctor telling me my test was positive. I decided to take a stab in the dark and see if my mum was at home. She was.

Inside, Mum asked how I was doing.

"Ok," I mumbled.

Mary's eyes narrowed. "Where have you been at this time in the morning?

"Doctors," I replied. I was aware I was giving one word answers but my head was a mess.

My mum came and sat beside me.

"You're pregnant, aren't you?" she said. I nodded.

"Does your father know?"

"Not yet, no-one knows, just you"

Having been pregnant 11 times herself, Mum knew how I was feeling. She smiled. "Your father isn't going to be happy about this." She said it in her usual sing-song voice. This was the way she always spoke. She had a lilt in her voice and it was rare you would hear her upset and angry. While she tried to keep that side of herself hidden, I can honestly say the only times I heard her angry was when she was fighting with her current partner.

Although I was worried about what Dad and my boyfriend would say, I felt ridiculously pleased Mum had that instinct to know what was wrong with her daughter. Deep down, I knew she wouldn't be there for me in my hour of need. It was only a matter of time before she disappeared again and I thought I'd be lucky to see her for the rest of my pregnancy.

In her flat that day, I decided to mine her for information on what to expect before that happened. I was quite scared but she soothed my fears and said, "There's nothing to it Gina. It's natural for women to have babies."

I wanted to retort, "It's also natural for a woman to stay with her babies," but of course I didn't.

She was curious about my boyfriend and I remember my eagerness to tell her all about him in the hope it would make her want to stick around and see more of me and meet him.

"Who is he, and what's he like?"

I told her he was handsome, had a full-time job and seemed to really like me. I said he was a decent laddie who wouldn't desert me just because I was pregnant.

She raised an eyebrow at that and said matter of factly, "I expect there will be a wedding then."

I shrugged. I really didn't know, I still had to tell him. And Dad.

"He said he would do the right thing by me."

I asked her what I should do. She gave a little shrug.

"Marry the laddie. It'll keep your father happy."

It's only now I realise she never mentioned my happiness – just my dad's. I'm not a psychologist but it seems to me that Mary probably never considered the welfare of her children at any point. I could be wrong. She wasn't even angry or upset that her teenage unmarried daughter was pregnant. And without even meeting my boyfriend first, her response was to marry him. I left her house that day and it was, as I suspected, a long time before I saw her again.

That night I told him about the baby.

His face dropped and he was far from happy, but it wasn't in his nature to shirk his responsibilities. He knew he wouldn't abandon me; times had not moved on that much. Unmarried mothers were still considered social pariahs even in the enlightened 70s.

We made plans to tell his mum and my dad. I wasn't looking forward to that at all. I was expecting hell fire and brimstone from wee Joe.

Saturday morning came around and I sought dad out in the pub. I was nervous. He didn't seem to pick up on that at all. He was more interested in his coupon. It took me a little while to pluck up the courage to say the words.

"Dad, I need to tell you something."

He didn't even look up, he was reading the newspaper in front of him.

"Dad..." I persisted. Eventually, he said, "Aye, what is it hen?"

I told him I was pregnant.

"Who's the father?"

"My boyfriend." Dad hadn't met him but I'd spoken about him briefly sometimes. I never really wanted to make a big deal out of having a boyfriend because I was worried about Dad's reaction.

"You will be getting married." That wasn't a question. I had no doubt that even if he had to carry me down the aisle myself I was getting married whether I wanted to or not.

Dad met my boyfriend for the first time at his parents

house in Milton, Glasgow. The parents had decided a meeting was in order to sort out arrangements for our wedding which would take place before I started showing my pregnancy.

Dad liked him instantly and I felt like I could breathe easily for the first time. Dad's approval meant everything to me and I thought if he likes him, my life will be so much easier. That evening they spoke for ages and he was able to charm my dad as much as he'd first charmed me.

His mother, Marie, was a sweet wonderful woman of Irish descent. A mother-of-nine, nothing was too much trouble for her family. I felt a little envious of him having such a devoted mother and I think she sensed my sadness at not having a mum around myself and also my fear of the unknown about what was going to happen to me during my pregnancy.

She took me under her wing and welcomed me into her family with open arms.

It was decided that Marie would arrange the wedding and she organised for us to go see the priest about our marriage ceremony. Coming from Catholic families, there was never any talk of anything but a wedding in the chapel.

The priest insisted my fiancé and I met with him several times to discuss what marriage meant according to the church. During our visits to the priest, who we nicknamed Father Uh Huh on account that he pulled my fiancé up for saying uh huh a few times , we were reminded marriage was for life and we had to live according to the rules of the holy Catholic Church. Father Uh Huh made us both attend confession to have our sin of sex outside marriage forgiven.

He spoke mostly to my fiancé and the conversation went like this:

"Do you understand what marriage is?"

"Uh-huh, father," he replied.

"Do you realise that it's a commitment for one man to stay faithful to one woman for the rest of his life?"

"Uh huh Father"

"Do you understand that you will bring all your children up in accordance with the teachings of the Catholic Church?"

"Uh huh, Father."

"Do you go to mass on a Sunday?"

"Uh huh, Father."

"Do you know any other words, other than 'uh huh?'"

"Uh huh, er, I mean, yes, Father." I could see he was dying to burst out laughing.

The priest turned to me and said, "Do you understand all of this?"

I nodded.

He tutted and said, "I would marry you but you are not in the catchment area for this Chapel, if you go and see the Father in Our Lady of the Assumption, I will tell him you have been to speak with me and that he should marry you both in his church."

We said our thanks and left, but once outside we burst into hysterical laughter.

I asked him if he wanted to go for a drink and he replied, "Uh huh."

Despite the hilarity of that day, I remember feeling quite anxious about the whole religious thing and worrying if I would go to hell, but he seemed to take it in his stride and told me not to worry about it. He said getting married meant I wouldn't go to hell for having sex with him.

6

Marriage and Maryhill

ON OCTOBER 3, 1970, while five months pregnant at 16 years old, we married in the Our Lady of the Assumption Catholic church in Bilsland Drive, Ruchill. I wore a white satin two-piece suit (only virgins were allowed to marry in white dresses) and a navy floppy hat, navy shoes and gloves.

He wore a navy-blue suit. I thought we both looked very smart.

The fact I was wearing a suit would have had local tongues wagging. I wasn't 'intact'. I'm pretty sure bets would have been taken whether I was pregnant or not.

We had the reception at his parents' home. His mum was an employee of City Bakeries so she managed to get a lot of food 'cheap' with a staff discount. My new husband and his brothers and sisters provided alcohol for the guests.

I heard Dad saying to him, "She will make you a very good wife, she is good at cooking and cleaning." And I remember thinking to myself, 'my God, I'm worth more than that!'

It was a side to Dad I didn't know existed if I'm honest. It made me think that perhaps Mum left because of Dad's attitude towards women. But he wasn't unusual in that respect, even today women are still regarded as the primary domestic homemakers, cooks, cleaners, bottle washers.

Of course, Dad came to the wedding and 'gave me away'. Mum didn't. I couldn't find her and nobody knew where she was in time for the wedding day. I felt quite down about it but it was another reminder my mum was a nomad who did what she wanted to do. Clearly attending her daughter's wedding was not on her list of priorities. It's probably just as well I didn't know where she was as Dad had already told me not to invite her. It would've put me in a terrible quandary as I was a good girl and did as I was told but I would've been tempted to invite my mum.

I think the person I am now would've told Dad to mind his own business and I could invite who I wanted to my own wedding. Thankfully we never had to have that kind of conversation.

I felt very content in my little newlywed bubble.

MARRIAGE AND MARYHILL

Our first house together was in Saracen Street and it had a pub underneath. We managed to get it because every day I walked daily from Maryhill to Partick to the lettings office to ask if there were any properties available. I did this for weeks and was beginning to look heavily pregnant.

One day I went in and the woman who worked there took me aside and said there was to be a set of keys handed in the next day and if I was early I would be in the queue first. She said if I came back with the advance rent money she would keep the key for me. I think she felt sorry for me. I was outside that office first thing the next morning and we were able to get our first house. I was absolutely delighted. We lived on the top floor so it wasn't so noisy. It was nothing more than a bedsit really with one room and a kitchen, a bedroom and a bathroom, which we furnished with gifts from his family and second hand furniture.

I was looking forward to married life and settling down even though I was only 16. The same couldn't be said for my new husband. He changed almost as soon as the ring was on my finger. He became moody and angry and told me he didn't even like children and everyone in his family knew that. It was said in an accusatory tone, as if I'd trapped him, but I felt I needed to point out he was the one who promised to stand by me when he wanted sex.

And so I spent a lot of time on my own while he was

in the pub after work and at the weekends. If I complained he would hit me. Usually when he was drunk and the next day he would be full of apologies and remorse.

On December 30th 1970, I gave birth to a beautiful baby girl. My husband , who didn't like children, was 'over the moon'. It was the day before Hogmanay which meant a double celebration for him.

On New Year's Day I remember looking around at all the other new mums surrounded by visitors and there was me on my own. No husband or family. I became distressed so they sedated me to send me back to sleep.

The next night he arrived looking sheepish. He had his dad with him. He apologised for not being in to see me or the baby. His excuse wasn't what I was expecting at all. He said there had been a terrible accident at a football game between Rangers FC and Celtic FC. They are the two biggest clubs in Glasgow and have a fierce rivalry dating back many many years.

People call them the 'Old Firm'. I believe that term came from an old cartoon which showed an elderly man selling sandwiches before the 1904 Scottish Cup Final with the sign 'Patronise The Old Firm: Rangers, Celtic Ltd'. Others say the term originated from commentators who said the teams were "like two old, firm friends" during an early match between the two.

Anyway, he said lots of people had been killed or injured after Ibrox stadium, which belonged to Rangers, collapsed. It later transpired the disaster, in which 66 people died and more than 200 people were injured, happened due to a crowd crush on a stairwell.

He said his brothers had been at the game and there were concerns about them. I remember feeling very sad for the loss of life but at the same time angry with him that he was using an awful tragedy to cover up for the fact he had spent two days drinking.

This was the start of my marriage problems. While my husband loved our daughter and was happy to take her out in her pram showing her off, he wasn't the best at honouring his vows. Love, cherish and be faithful for the rest of his life seemed to be forgotten very quickly. I was desperate to have a happy home and tried my best even though he beat me quite often when he was drunk. Alcohol seemed to turn my 'great guy' of a husband into a monster.

One thing he homed in on was how insecure I was about a port wine birthmark on my face. It covered my left cheek and I had spent all of my life feeling as if I was ugly and mocked by other children. In adulthood, I was always particular about my appearance. I grew my hair waist length and it was always impeccably groomed. I dressed well and ensured my children were always perfect.

When he came home in a drunken rage, accusing me of affairs with imaginary men, he would drag me to the mirror and tell me to be thankful he'd taken me because I was so ugly no one else would want me with a face like that. I didn't suffer in silence and often answered him back which would earn me a slap across the face if not worse.

I had nowhere to go and no-one to turn to. I longed for my mother but oftentimes she was in the wind and I had no idea where she was. There was no point crying to my dad who was of the opinion there was nothing wrong with a slap now and then to keep your woman in line. And he would've been heartbroken to learn how sad and miserable I was married to this man.

The only thing I could do was throw my energy into my children. We eventually went on to have three, Laura, Gail and Joseph. I tried my best to hide the violence from them and would often muffle the sounds of my tears after another beating in the vain hope they wouldn't know about it.

A few months after our wedding, Dad came to visit me with a present. He had not been able to get us a wedding gift at the time but on this visit he turned up with a boxed cutlery set. He said this is your wedding present and sorry I couldn't buy it at the time. I could tell he was gearing up to ask me something and waited.

He said it's no longer possible for me to stay at your

uncle's house as one of the older boys got married and he and his wife are moving in until they can find a home of their own.

"Can I come and stay with you for a bit?"

He lived with us for a few months until he found another house in Partick. As cramped as we were, I loved having my dad staying with us. As far as my dad was concerned, we were a very happily married couple.

We moved houses a lot and eventually had enough money to put down a deposit on a flat. I was aged 22 by then and we had two daughters.

At that time there was an abundance of private sellers. You paid a deposit and a monthly amount until the balance was paid in full. There was no such thing as a mortgage.

The flat was on the corner of Garrioch Road and Stratford Street. It was known as North Kelvinside, when in fact it was really Maryhill. People who rented their flats called it Maryhill area, those who were buying them called it North Kelvinside.

I remember attending a meeting with the local authority and the residents of the area to determine if it was Maryhill or North Kelvinside. Looking back, it was quite ridiculous, but it was a particularly important issue to some people at the time. What area you lived in determined how affluent you were. Such snobbery still exists to this day.

Over the years, Dad would visit twice a week. If he could not manage, I would go to him. He was proud to show off his daughter and grandchildren to his friends. Sometimes in the evenings he visited he would ask if I'd seen my sisters. And this was always followed up with, "I did my best bringing you all up."

With an outstretched hand he would hand me an empty whisky glass from his jacket pocket and ask if I had any. Of course he knew I did because there was always whisky in the house for my husband. Dad, whisky in hand, would start a singsong. Always love songs. One of his favourites was 'On The Street Where You Live' from the 1956 musical 'My Fair Lady'.

"That was my song to your mother," and his eyes would fill up with tears. I'd tell him not to get morbid and he'd burst into another song. He sang 'Show Me the Way to Go Home' by Irving King.

I would cut in and say it's time to go home dad and he'd ask to stay the night. He'd fall asleep on the chair and I'd take off his shoes, loosen his tie and throw a blanket over him. It was a ritual I had done since I was seven years old, but these days there was one extra task; I'd gently shake him and say, 'Dad, give me your teeth out, I don't want you to choke.' He'd purse his lips together and push out his teeth. An art he'd obviously mastered.

After he died, I'd have given anything for one last

singsong at my house or one last purse of his lips to give me his teeth, no matter how much both those things irritated me at the time.

It's true what they say, sometimes you don't know the value of a moment until it's gone.

Dad always spent Christmas and New Year with me. When pub licensing laws changed to all day opening he did not come so often, preferring the company of his pals in the pub until the wee small hours. When he did visit he would tease the children and squeeze their nose in a fun way.

I often heard loud squeals from one of the children, "Ouch, mum, Granda's pinching my nose, it hurts."

He would laugh at the tips of their noses being red, but this was his way of showing them affection and love.

A lot happened for me personally over the years I spent with my husband. I did some psychiatric nurse training. I had another child and moved into a social work job. My marriage was very troubled and not how I imagined it to be. I lived in a pink world. I wanted life to be a fairy tale. I wanted a life that was different to that of my mum and dad.

My relationship was breaking down. In actual fact, it was probably breaking down from the very first moment he lifted his hands to me. I always knew it wasn't going to end well. The turning point came when our oldest daughter, Laura, who was 15 at the time, told me the children had seen and heard more than they had let on. She said enough was enough.

"Don't let my wee brother see or hear what me and my sister have had to listen to for the past ten years. You might not think we heard or seen and you might think you covered it up but we have heard and seen more than you think."

I could no longer keep it a secret from Dad. I told him the truth. He was devastated and asked why I hadn't told him.

"How could I? We are Catholics, Dad, and what could you have done? I was embarrassed and wanted to keep my family together. Everyone is scattered and none of us have any stability in our lives."

Little did I know that fate was about to throw further shocks at me that would eclipse my crumbling marriage.

7

Memories of my Mum

"YOU CAN'T stay here anymore, Gina, your mother has legged it again."

The words of my stepfather, John, rang loudly in my ears as I tearfully walked the four-mile journey from Maryhill in the North-west of Glasgow to Drumchapel where my older sister, Carol, was living at the time.

It might have been summertime but my body was chilled to the bone thanks to spending the previous night sleeping in a stairwell outside.

My life felt like it was falling apart. Actually, it didn't feel like it, it *was* falling to pieces. Crumbling, disintegrating, going to rack and ruin. My dad was living with his brother, my siblings were scattered over Glasgow and Mum had done another disappearing act.

I was on my own. It was July 1969.

I remember the date because Buzz Aldrin had just walked on the moon and the whole world was electrified with excitement and the wonder of the possibilities open to mankind. A man on the moon! It was incredible, but while America was feeling exuberant and literally on top of the world, life in Glasgow hadn't changed.

In fact, America might as well have been on another planet as far as the ordinary man on the street was concerned. More specifically, 15-year-old me.

History being made on the other side of the pond did not make a blind bit of difference to my existence. While some of my peers might have been dreaming of flying to the stars or discovering the next cure for disease, as I lay on a stone-cold floor huddled underneath an old flea-riddled fur coat for warmth, my dreams were a little more basic. I just wanted a family. A home with heat, food and lighting. And a mother. A caring and devoted mother. I would've been more successful shooting for the moon.

As you've probably realised by now, my relationship with my mum is complicated. This was not her first, nor her last disappearing act.

Since I was a little girl, my mum has been walking in and out of my life as if it were a revolving door. Years could roll by where I didn't see Mum then one day I'd bump into her on the street, and she would glide back into my life as if she'd never been away. My memories of her are very obscure and I didn't think there were many at all, but when I dug deep I discovered there were actually more than I thought. Some of them are not so great recollections but others make me smile.

I am telling these stories not to sully her memory or make her sound bad but to be honest and lay demons to rest.

Some of the way parents behaved in my time would be frowned upon now and regarded as neglect or child abuse, but this would mean that most of my generation were abused children. It's cliched but true — it's just the way things were then. We didn't know any different, we weren't as enlightened as we are now about dysfunctional childhoods or parenting.

Poverty played a huge role in how people lived their lives but we also snatched pleasure whenever we could: going to the pub or dances or, if you were feeling really flush, the cinema. Dining out, going to the theatre and music concerts were for people with money.

It sounds like I'm excusing my parents' generation for their behaviour, but they learned from their parents before them and so forth. Granted, Mum was a law unto herself. Not many women had the courage to walk out on their families. Sometimes she would come back for a week or two but her and dad would fight again and one of them would disappear.

My earliest memory of this is a time, I was around

five or six years old, when Dad had walked out and Mum was back for a few days. I was off school for some reason and lying in bed. The sheet was filthy. Two of my aunts came to visit and were in the living room with Mum when Dad came in. I could hear a very heated exchange going on and my dad was asking why I wasn't at school and why I was lying in filth. He was furious.

He came into the room and told me to get dressed. I was very embarrassed and to this day I still remember it because the fight escalated to a physical altercation between him and the three women and he was put out of the house. I remember chasing him up the street crying for him to take me with him. He told me to go back as he got on the bus.

My heart still aches to this day when I think of it. My poor gentle Dad. Mum and the two aunts had really given him a beating and he had refused to fight back.

He came back a week later and Mum was furious. She didn't want to stay in the house with him so she left. I have no idea where she went, I just remember it was a long time before I saw her again.

There was another time, I'm not sure how old I was, when I was playing outside and another child said to me your mum is lying in the field sleeping. The field – which we called Bluebell Woods – was behind the school on my street so I made my way up there.

She was curled up in a ball and looked dishevelled.

I shook her awake. I remember thinking she's not sleeping, she's dead, but then she sat up and said my name. Her first question to me was to ask if my dad was angry, but I didn't know what she was talking about and said so. She told me to go back home so I ran down to the house and told Dad Mum was in the field. That night she came and stayed and was there for a few days before she disappeared again.

A few years later, when my sister Carol was living in a convent, Mum was going to visit and asked if I wanted to go with her. I was so happy to be doing something with Mum but also because I missed my sister and was excited to see her again.

Just before we got in Mum asked if I would hide a packet of cigarettes in my sock which came up to my knee. Because I was a child, she said, I wouldn't be searched but she would be. Carol was caught with them later by the nuns who confiscated them, and I was banned from ever visiting my sister again!

When Mum had the twins, Brian and David, to John Cullen, I visited her in the Queen Mother hospital in Yorkhill. I was so happy to see her. I took her a box of Malteser chocolates and helped her eat them. She asked me if I would like to give the boys their names. I was only 12 and it meant the world to me that she asked me to do this for her.

A few years later I was living in Possilpark at the time

MY MOTHER'S MURDER

and Mum was living nearby in Keppochill. I would sometimes walk over to her house and spend some time with her. I was a new mum by then, and my daughter Laura was around five months old when she became unwell and was crying a lot. I needed my mum. I didn't know what to do with this child who wouldn't stop crying.

Mum was back in her house with John at the time and they were huddled around the coal fire. Laura would just not stop crying so mum said to hand her over to her.

"She sounds like she's got wind, Gina, give her to me." I watched as mum heated a small pot of water over the fire and once it cooled she gave it to my daughter. A few minutes later my daughter burped and settled for the first time in days. Another life lesson from Mum.

When Mum moved from Keppochhill, a house in the building I was living in became vacant. I spoke to the factor and asked if my mum could rent it. It was the same size of house she already had but it did have the luxury of an inside toilet. I was so happy to have her close by.

There was one day my daughter was quite unwell. She was around nine-months old and was admitted to Stobhill hospital for around 10 days. When she was being discharged, mum went with me to pick her up. Laura wouldn't come to me, she wanted my mum. I remember Mum laughing about that and saying Laura was a 'granny's girl'.

I thought living in the same building we would see more of each other but that didn't happen. She was only there for a brief time with John and their children before they left.

I moved shortly after that to Maryhill and it was about another year and a half before I saw Mum again. By this time I had been accepted for a placement in psychiatric nursing.

One day on my way home from school, I bumped into Mum on the street. As usual there was no chat about how long it had been since we'd seen each other. Years could go by and she would act as if you'd just seen each other the day before. I was used to it by then.

She first asked how my husband and the kids were then she wanted to know about the folders under my arm. I told her I was training to be a nurse. She told me she'd briefly gone into nursing and was thinking of going back to it and could she borrow my notes to revise? She said she would apply when the course next came up. We arranged to meet for a coffee and I handed over my notes. She said she would see me soon to return them. It would be a number of years before I saw her again.

Every time she breezed back into our lives she wouldn't mention her long periods of absence. To her it was as normal as breathing. I couldn't imagine going for a few days without some form of contact with my children, let alone years. I think her mum dying young and her dad going off to sea left her with such trauma that she saw abandoning your loved ones as typical parenting. I know it sounds silly because her mum died and couldn't help it, but Mary was only five years old when that happened and I doubt anyone took the time to explain to the child why her mother was no longer around.

Children don't understand death. You could say to them, "your mum has gone to heaven to be with the angels" and I'm sure to a five-year-old that's just like saying "she's gone to the shops and she'll be back soon". Mary should have been treated with love and care and helped to understand why her life changed so much.

It's easy to say all of this in this day and age, now that we have a culture of social norms where talking about your emotions and feelings is considered healthy and therapeutic. Back in my mum's day, or even my day, it just wasn't the done thing. Life dealt you a rough hand and you just got on with it. Mum died on a Monday and you still had to go to work on a Tuesday, bereavement days off just didn't exist except for the funeral. It sounds harsh but it was true.

One time I met her at the bottom of Byres Road in Glasgow's West End and my father had seen us from a distance. Instead of just walking by or stopping to say hello, he jumped into the subway entrance and popped his head out to see if we'd left.

Later that day, my father asked me if I had seen my mother recently, I answered yes and so have you, why did you try to hide? I think he mumbled some excuse and changed the subject. They had not been together for 29 years but there was some complicated connection between them that continued until death. I think my dad did love my mum, until his dying day, and it's probably why we never saw him with another woman. There wasn't anyone who could hold a candle to Mary.

I make it sound like Mary was a terrible mother, don't I? I can only offer up my experiences with her and our relationship. Despite the fact she abandoned me I still felt a deep love for her, and to this day I still do. I may not have known her really but it feels instinctive of a child to love their mother. Mum died when I was 30 and it makes me sad to think how few memories I have of her. I'm sure, buried deep down, I have many more but maybe that's just a fantasy I tell myself because the reality is that I didn't really know her at all and our sporadic contact is more proof of that.

My children probably have funnier and happier memories of Mum than I do. With her grandchildren she was able to let go and show her childish side much more than she could with her own children.

Gail remembers her Granny Mary as being funny and always having packets of Tootie Fruity sweets for her and her sister. She said she remembers her Granny's yellow-stained fingertips from smoking rolled up Woodbine cigarettes. She was always laughing and joking. Gail told me about the time Mum spotted a rose in one of my vases and asked Gail to give her it as a gift but not to tell me or her dad. How cheeky, but so typical of Mum.

She tried to tempt Gail into staying overnight once by saying she had chocolate biscuits in the cupboard.

But the funniest moment for Gail was when she had to hunt down her Granny in a pub and all Mum's friends came out to say hello. One of them tried to give Gail a £5 note and she said it was too much and refused to take it. Mum promptly took the note from the man's outstretched hand and stuffed it down her bra.

My oldest daughter, Laura, loves to tell her own children the stories about their great-grandmother such as the time when she visited just after Christmas the year they got roller skates from Santa. The conversation went like this:

"What did Santa bring you then, girls?"

The girls, aged eight and 10, looked at their Gran as if she was a toddler.

"We know Santa is not real, Gran, it's your mum and dad," they said.

Mary replied, "Of course he's real."

The girls turned to me and Laura said, "Mum, guess what? Gran is like 1,000 years old and she doesn't know that it isn't really Santa Claus."

They were giggling when Mary said, "Haud yer wheesht, and let me see what you got."

Mum was particularly interested in their skates – roller disco boots they were called.

"What size are they? I was a good skater when I was young. Let me have a shot."

Mum had drunk a small whisky so the girls were a bit concerned and told her so.

"It's been raining Granny, and you've got Mum's silk dress on." It was really a kaftan I'd given her while her own clothes were drying from the rain.

She insisted she was such a good skater, the girls had to come see for themselves.

She put the boots on and unbelievably within a few minutes she was whizzing up and down the hallway. I could hear their squeals of laughter from the kitchen.

It was a long time before Laura and Gail saw their 'roller skating granny' again. The years passed and the girls were teenagers before Mary came to visit.

"You're grown up now, Laura, you look like your Da. And you, Gail, you still have a wee cheeky bugger look about you."

She invited Laura to tea at her house a few days later

and they arranged to meet at 4pm at Partick Cross. As usual, Mum was late, and the girls were getting anxious. An old lady with white hair walked towards them and Laura's friend asked if that was her.

Laura giggled, "That's nothing like my Granny. There she is now." She pointed to Mum and Alison's mouth opened wide in shock.

Mum's carrot red hair was a sight to behold along with her yellow and green Glasgow Celtic poncho, jeans and plimsoles. My mother was no member of the blue rinse brigade that's for sure.

She told the girls she wasn't in the mood for cooking so took them to the chip shop. Alison had remained mute.

Mary said, "Has the cat got your tongue?"

"She's just shy, Granny."

"Listen," she said, "when we get to the chippy, just tell them you're my niece. No-one knows I'm a granny."

Laura could only laugh, but Alison was silent.

As they sat in Mum's house eating, Mary offered the girls a cigarette.

"I won't tell your ma," she said. They both refused. Alison was looking at Mary as if she'd come from another planet.

She gave them a pound each to spend at the shops and they walked her to the pub.

"Thanks for coming to see me, I'll see you again soon." She left them standing outside.

Alison finally spoke.

"I thought you were kidding when you said that was your Granny, I have never seen a Granny like that before."

Laura replied, "Neither have I."

Granny Mary was the highlight of their day and the topic of their conversation for months to come.

8

The Grim Reaper

IT WAS a quiet morning in 1984 when, after sending my children off to school, I suddenly realised I hadn't heard from Dad for a few days which was unusual. He didn't have a house phone so I called my sister Margaret to ask if she'd seen him. She told me he had been staying at her house in Clydebank for a few days but hadn't been feeling well so he decided to go back to his own house. She said he'd become incontinent and this was upsetting him.

I remember saying to her, "He must be dying."

"Oh, don't say that Gina," she replied.

She said he had seemed brighter when he left to go home to collect his pension.

That calmed me down and I expected him to come for his usual weekend visit but he didn't appear. I thought about going to the pub to see him but I had a lot on with the children and work and before I knew it the weekend was over and it was back to a busy week of juggling school, work, cooking and cleaning.

By the Wednesday I was anxious. It really was now an overly long time without seeing my dad. Margaret hadn't seen him either. I asked Laura to pop to his house on the way home from school but she came back and said he wasn't in the house, the bookies or the pub.

He had a lady friend, an Irish woman, who lived in Church Street and quite often he would go for tea at her house so I reasoned that perhaps he had gone there. He often took her little boy to nursery and always chuckled at the fact the boy couldn't pronounce 'Wee Joe' and would call him 'Wee Doe'.

On Friday, 7 September 1984, I was in the house catching up on some housework when the phone rang. It was my sister Kathleen.

She'd been to Dad's house and couldn't get an answer at the door so she looked in the window and could see him lying in front of the fireplace. The window was open a little, so she was able to crank it wide enough to get inside.

"I think he's dead," she said. "A heart attack. The neighbour let me use her phone to call the police and ambulance." Her tone was matter of fact.

I was shocked. I burst into tears and, trembling, I

called my brother, John, down south immediately. He said he would come straight away.

An hour later I was at Dad's house and met by a police officer. Margaret arrived soon after. The police arranged for dad's body to be removed from his house and later they told us there were no suspicious circumstances. They had verified with his family doctor that Dad had been attending the surgery within three months of his death and was being treated for alcoholic colitis. This was a complete surprise to me as Dad hadn't mentioned it all and he usually told me everything.

The police said the Crown Office didn't require a post-mortem so his death certificate could be issued. There was also talk that Dad seemed to have fallen and when he couldn't get back up he choked on his own vomit.

I don't know what they put on the death certificate for cause of death. I've always found it too difficult to look at. Does it matter anyway? Dead is dead regardless. My poor Daddy.

Communicating bad news in 1984 was not as easy as it is today. Mobile phones, of course, didn't exist and a lot of families were scattered. Those of us who lived nearby gathered in my house while we contacted as many family members as we could. The older siblings were discussing the funeral arrangements and I remember I was so distraught at his death that I couldn't think straight.

I refused to have his body back to my house for the Catholic ritual of a 'vigil' where family and friends can gather round an open or closed casket while a priest leads prayer. Some people call it the 'wake'.

I couldn't cope with the thought of him in my house with lots of people coming in and out. It was decided the vigil would be done at the funeral parlour and Dad's burial would be held at St Simon's Chapel in Partickbridge Street.

On the eve of his funeral, my half-brother, Martin, came to my house and said Mum was outside in a car. My older sister and brother went out to speak to her to tell her she could not travel with the family to the funeral. There were a lot of bitter feelings towards Mum.

I couldn't bear the thought of my beloved dad going into the cold ground. I almost backed out of going to the burial. I remember being given a large brandy to calm my nerves. It seemed to work because in the chapel I was quite at ease. It was standing room only. Wee Joe had been a popular character in Partick.

The service was conducted by Father Tierney and as we left to go to the graveside, I looked over and saw the slight figure of my mother peering through the sea of faces. I wanted to cry out to her to come beside me. She looked so sad and lonely standing there. I was ushered into the car and the moment passed. Another missed opportunity to connect with her.

During the 'purvey' – some people call it the funeral wake or reception – my brother, John, who'd had a few whiskeys, said he needed to tell me something.

John said Dad had made him promise just weeks before he died that if anything ever happened to him, he was to make sure my mother never got the house.

"She won't want to take it anyway," I said. I was confused but the conversation was happening so fast. What he told me next is etched on my mind forever.

"You know they never divorced, right? That means she's entitled to the house."

"I don't think she would want it," I insisted. I felt a strong need to defend her. "Give her some credit," I added.

He puffed up a little and told me, "I can never allow that to happen. I promised Dad I would make sure she didn't get it and will do whatever was in my power to stop her if she tried."

Instead of thinking about what John was saying to me, my mind drifted. I wonder, even to this day, if Dad knew he was dying and this is why he had that conversation with John.

"This is just the drink talking. The house is in a bad condition and needs refurbished. It's not worth much and Mum wouldn't have the money to decorate it anyway." I closed the conversation down and didn't think much more about it.

But what unfolded over the next few weeks was rather distasteful and disgusting.

Dad's house was a one-room apartment. He had been gifted it a few years before by a friend. The friend who had heard Dad was homeless insisted Dad move in and all he had to pay was the legal fees for the transfer of ownership. Dad died without a will so legally it belonged to Mum.

After Dad's funeral, I went to visit his sister, my auntie Cathie. I had not seen her since I was a child. She lived in the southside of Glasgow in Allison Street. She was in a melancholy mood and told me some stories about my dad when he was a child. I was surprised to learn that his family called him 'Josie' and he was the baby of the family. She said he was a sickly child who was always clingy with his mother. It reminded me that part of his problem with my mum was his devotion to his mother.

Auntie Cathie said his marriage to Mum would never have worked for that reason.

"Women don't like to think they're competing with your mother or that you've only married them to replace her. Josie would always run to our mammy when life got too much for him but he was a good man yer da, so he was."

I asked Auntie Cathie what she thought of my mum.

"Wee Ginger is a funny one that's for sure. Aw you

weans and she couldn't hack it. Your da wouldn't have been much help either. I'm sure most of us would run away given half the chance. Fair play to her." She said this with a laugh.

Auntie Cathie died many years ago but I've never forgotten that conversation. I liked her and I wished she'd been around more when I was a child.

I met with Mum several times after Dad's funeral and of course the big topic of conversation was his flat. She told me she didn't want it and didn't understand why there would be drama over it.

She said, "Gina, I've been away from your dad for 29 years. Why would I want his hoose? It wouldn't be right if I took it and stopped his kids getting their inheritance. I'm no that bad!" She gave a wee chuckle at that.

While I was devastated over dad's death – I was after all a daddy's girl at heart – I felt I was at last beginning to form a relationship with my mother. It made me happy.

One day she called me to say she was outside his house as she had arranged to meet my sister, Kathleen, there. She said when she arrived, the door had been forced open. She didn't want to go in alone. Kathleen hadn't turned up and could I go down? When I arrived, Mum was upset.

She said she was sorry about his death and how things had turned out. While we waited for a key to arrive we had a surprising conversation. I didn't know it then, but it would be the most meaningful conversation I'd ever have with her.

It would also be our last.

She seemed melancholy, almost like guilt and regret was weighing heavily on her and she needed to unburden herself somehow. She said she was feeling sad and sorrowful about Dad dying but admitted she'd never loved him.

"I married him because John left me. I never loved Joe, but he was a good man. He knew I didn't love him, but he stayed, and he would've been happy to stay with me for the rest of his life. I feel bad about what happened, but my life wasn't good. I needed to leave. I am sorry for you that Joe is gone. He was a good dad to you all."

She then said something strange.

"Money was taken from your dad's pocket as he lay dead."

I was shocked and angry. I didn't know what to say. Mum admitted covering up for the person who took it because she felt sorry for them.

She added, "The police who attended when he died told her she could take it. It was Kathleen, Gina."

Mum told me Dad had been found at 8.30am and his pension was cashed at 9am. It was a weird confession, and I couldn't help but wonder what else Kathleen was getting up to. Was this a prophetic feeling about my sister? Kathleen spent the rest of her life denying she had cashed it and pocketed the money. Mum and I agreed to meet up another time for a coffee when the dust had settled. She said she would call me.

She was visibly upset and I tried to placate her as best as I could but I was grieving, my emotions were in turmoil and I couldn't think straight.

A few days later she called back but I wasn't available. My husband took the message.

"Tell Gina I have something to tell her, I will call her back," she said.

That call never came.

On October 2, 1984, just three weeks after we buried my dad, I was busy preparing dinner for my family when the phone rang.

Expecting it to be my husband to say he was either on his way home or working late, I was surprised to hear the voice of one of my siblings. There had been animosity at Dad's funeral. I braced myself for an argument. Martin was upset. His voice was shaky. I felt a stirring of alarm.

"Gina, I have just been to ma's, she's dead, she's been murdered."

Those words sent an icy chill through my body.

"The police are at my ma's flat now, when I went to her door, I didn't get an answer, I looked through the letter box. The lights and the central heating were on.

The smell was so bad I knew that something was very wrong. I kicked the door in and I found her body."

His words weren't sinking in. I was silent while my brain scrambled to process what he had just said. Then shock kicked in and I went into automatic pilot mode. Think, Gina, think!

I couldn't leave the children alone, my husband worked 10 minutes from our house and often stopped at the bookies on his way home. The thought of traipsing to a bookies to find my wayward husband to tell him such news was more than I could stand, so I phoned instead. I needed to catch him before he left. Luckily, I did. I had, in my head, rehearsed what I was going to say – something gentle and not too dramatic.

When he came to the phone the first words that came out my mouth were, "Mum has been murdered. You have to come straight home."

Whoever thinks they're going to have to tell people their mum was murdered?

Little did I know, I would spend decades saying it.

"Jesus, I will come now, I will get a lift," he said.

My head was bursting. I couldn't fathom it. Dad just died three weeks ago. Surely there was some mistake and it wasn't Mum?

Of course, he was full of questions when he arrived.

"I do not know, all I know is that she has been murdered. Martin phoned me to tell me."

I think in those situations our brains focus on trivial matters as a form of protection because as soon as I felt myself wallowing in the fact they were dead within weeks of each other. I started talking about looking after the kids.

"Dinner is ready, the children have not eaten yet, can you see to it that they do their homework? I don't know how long I will be out. After that, Laura is going to her friend's house for a little while."

As I went from room to room getting my things together, he was following me asking questions I could not answer. It was a cold, wet night so I was thinking I should take a hat with me.

"I'll need to go and tell Kathleen," I was more speaking my thoughts out loud than to my husband.

"I'll take a taxi; I'm not walking for 20 minutes in the rain."

When I arrived at Kathleen's home, her long-term partner was there. Their set-up was probably weird to most people. You see, he was her partner, but he didn't live with her. They would spend morning until night together then he would go home to his wife. His wife knew about Kathleen and seemed to accept the situation.

Usually, I was greeted quite warmly whenever I visited but this was no ordinary visit and Kathleen seemed to instinctively know something was very wrong. I told her to sit down. Her face paled.

"What is it? It's my ma isn't it? She's dead."

There was no way of softening the blow.

"Yes," I replied. "She's been murdered, and we need to go to her house."

My matter-of-fact manner I now know was probably a stress reaction. I was trying to stay calm in the face of an unfamiliar world. I was grappling with the fact I truly was an orphan now; Mum and Dad's faces were swirling around in my brain. I told Kathleen that Martin Cullen had found her body.

"Police are there now; we need to go."

Kathleen's face was devoid of colour and for someone who usually had plenty to say she was surprisingly silent. Her partner didn't say much either as she got herself organised.

We got a taxi. Nothing was said between us. But to be honest what could we say? We didn't know any facts yet and we were numb. We could see a police officer standing at the front door of the third floor flat from the road.

People were leaning out of their flat windows, some had gathered on the street whispering and pointing. I'm sure word would have gone round quickly that someone was dead and the police presence would confirm this was no ordinary death.

Of course we weren't allowed in the house.

The officer took out his little black book and took our

details. He then radioed the office and told us to wait until a police car came to take us to the station.

"You'll need to attend the station down in Gullane Street. The Marine office." He didn't look us in the eye. The officer was all business and very brusque, there was no compassion or sympathy at all. His job was merely to guard the scene and stop anyone entering the flats.

I would like to think that relatives of murder victims are treated far more sensitively nowadays. Back then it wasn't a word in police vocabulary. It was official. Mum really had been murdered and detectives were hunting for her killer.

9

A Callous Killer

THE POLICE didn't hang about.

Very quickly a cabin was set up outside Mum's building. If people didn't know a murder had occurred before, they most certainly did now.

As Kathleen and I stood waiting in the cold waiting for the police car to come and collect us, I looked up at Mum's window.

"My mother is lying in there, dead," I thought. I shivered involuntarily. Kathleen huddled next to me and grabbed my arm.

"Look at them aw, come for a neb." She pointed to the people gathered as police officers tried to shoo away nosy neighbours and passers-by. Children had appeared to gawk at the spectacle opening up before their very eyes.

An ambulance pulled up with blue lights and I

remember thinking that was stupid because she was already dead so what was the rush?

People came out of their houses, hanging out of their windows all pointing and staring. I felt my body shrink. I wanted to disappear. The police officer looked uncomfortable. I was aware I was gripping onto Kathleen. We were soaked through.

I couldn't allow myself to think about how she'd died, I didn't want to let my mind go there but it betrayed me and I started to conjure up all sorts of horrors about what she might have endured. Wee Mary. Ginger Murphy. Never hurt a soul – not physically anyway – happy Wee Mary, everybody's pal… lying dead in her own home having been murdered.

Another cabin arrived. More police officers. More reminders to everyone that wee Mary McLaughlin was dead. I wanted to run away. This couldn't be happening. I should be at home putting my children to bed, sorting out their school clothes for tomorrow, I thought. Instead I'm standing here in the pouring rain and freezing cold because they've said my mother has been murdered.

I made a funny sound but I wasn't aware of it until Kathleen shook my arm.

"Gina, whit ye dain?" Her eyes looked like flying saucers in the dark. I gave a little giggle. It's what Mum would've done, I thought.

Kathleen tutted and turned away.

"Where's this fucking police car?" She wasn't speaking to anyone in particular. Which was fine because nobody answered anyway. At last, the police car arrived to take us away from this circus. All I could feel was relief as the driver pulled away.

Kathleen and I didn't utter a word the whole journey. We were too consumed in our own thoughts, too shocked, I guess, at the nightmare we found ourselves in.

At the station it was absolute bedlam. You'd think in a city used to murder they would be better prepared for families arriving but then I guess Mary McLaughlin had a bigger family than most.

Some of my other siblings were already at the station. We were shoved into a room big enough to accommodate us all and someone came and said our fingerprints would need to be taken. For elimination purposes, they added.

I can't remember who was all there. I just remember a blur of faces, some crying and some pale and quiet. At some point someone else came and said everyone would have to give statements especially about their movements in the days and hours before Mary died. They obviously knew from the decomposition of the body that she had been dead a while and I now know they instantly ruled her death as a murder due to the fact the weapon was still around her neck.

I remember babbling to the officer who was taking my fingerprints. I had found my voice but I wasn't making any sense. I was mumbling about the comedy magician Tommy Cooper. Cooper was a large lumbering fez-wearing comic whose shtick was failed magic tricks and a catchphrase 'Just like that' where he would spread out his hands and jerk them in front of his body. He was hugely popular in the 70s and 80s. He had died earlier in 1984.

The ink from the fingerprint pad was all over the tips of my fingers and I remember looking down and suddenly I shouted, "How did Tommy Cooper die? Just like that!" I tried to imitate his voice as well as the actions.

Nobody laughed. I knew I was doing it, I was aware it was hysteria but I couldn't control it nor stop myself from doing it. I continued with my Cooper joke a few times until a kind police officer or clerical worker gently led me to the bathroom to wash off the ink. It seemed to snap me out of my temporary madness.

She led me back to a seat. My dad just died, I told her. How can my mother be dead too? They're both dead. I felt hysteria welling up again in my throat and I had to clamp my teeth almost over my tongue to keep from crying out. I heard someone sobbing in the background. I didn't look to see who. It might not have even been someone crying for Mary.

I'm an orphan already. It was like a broken record running through my mind. How could this be? Why God, why?

We sat about the station waiting to be told we were free to go. My daughter, Laura, arrived soon after. She was only 14 but they wanted her fingerprints too, to rule her out as a suspect. I felt a bubble of hysterical laughter erupt in my throat. Laura! An innocent child being considered, albeit briefly, as a suspect in her own grandmother's murder. I was aware on some level that all of us were suspects until we could be ruled out. What bastard had brought this evil into our lives?

I had to get Laura out of there. I had to get out. I'd never been involved with the police in my life. I felt nervous and scared. I knew much worse was still to come. I think I told Kathleen I was taking my child home. She looked pale and, for once in her life, quiet. She just nodded and looked away.

My husband was waiting for us when we arrived home. I've no idea what time it was, it was as if all the clocks had stopped and the world was no longer turning.

"How are you?" he asked, "Would you like a cup of tea, or something stronger?

"A whiskey, make it a large one." I replied.

He went through to the kitchen and brought two large glasses of whiskey.

He told me the two younger children had done their

homework and were asleep. He had left out their clean clothes for school in the morning. He was like that sober: a good caring husband and a great guy to be around.

Laura was exhausted and went to bed and he asked what had happened at the station.

"We all had to give our fingerprints. They want to know where everyone was and someone will be coming to take statements from us all."

"All of you? That's going to take a while," he replied.

"Have they given you any information at all? How she died? How do they know it's murder?"

I sighed. There was that word again. It sent a shiver through me. His curiosity was normal but I felt irritated.

"I've no idea," I snapped. "They didn't tell us anything at all. She's still in her flat so they probably don't know themselves." He got up and switched on the television. The late news headlines were on. I was unprepared. There, staring back at me was my mother's face. Her murder had already made the television news. All I heard was the newsreader saying 'a woman has been found…' I couldn't listen anymore. How was this possible the media knew already? Some of her family were still at the police station, for God's sake!

I wasn't even sure if anyone had notified her partner, Terry. He was working away in Oban.

The reality of what was happening hit home. There

would be a big investigation, another funeral and finding out who killed her and why.

It was all very overwhelming. I was just beginning to have my mother back in my life, we were finally beginning to discover who we were as people, as a mother and a daughter, dipping our toes into the water to see how our relationship would pan out. I thought I would have more time. She's gone away again but now she's gone for good. She is never coming back.

A memory came to me in that moment. It was at least 10 years before the tragedy and I had bumped into her in the street. As always, I invited her over for dinner. She turned up late but I wasn't bothered about that, at least this time she had shown up because many times before she hadn't. It was a Saturday and I had said to her, be at mine for 5pm, but it was around 6pm before she showed. She was quite tipsy with a few whiskeys already in her.

My husband, who wouldn't usually be home until after the bookies had closed, was home and the children were playing in their bedroom. He was just moaning about her tardiness and how hungry he was when she came in.

She was almost singing the words 'I am here', one hand clutching the handrail and the other a carrier bag.

"I'm a wee bit late, hen. I was bought a few whiskeys in the pub and you know me, I can't walk away and leave them. I told the barman to put them behind the gantry and I'll get them later." She was laughing at this, as if the idea she had drink waiting for her back at the pub was amusing. She walked into the living room and gave him a hard slap on the back of his head. It was meant to be friendly.

"What's that you're drinking? I'll have one." She nodded to his carryout bag sitting at his side. "Guid day at the horses then?"

She opened a can of beer and he asked if she wanted a glass and she howled with laughter.

"Don't be daft! Why would I bother with a glass," she said. She produced chocolate from her bag and said it was for the kids. She asked what we were having for dinner.

"Steak pie and lentil soup," I said.

"Can I just have the soup, hen? I'm no that hungry." She sat at the table and lit a cigarette. The children stared at her silently.

"Cat got your tongues?" she laughed again. She picked up a saucer at the same time asking if I had an ashtray. "No matter, this will do." Another sing-song voice.

She started to eat her soup but the next thing she was choking. Huge big gulping breaths and her face was going beetroot. I slapped her back, gave her a drink of water but she still had difficulty catching her breath and was coughing. She said she didn't feel too good.

I said we should go to the hospital and she agreed. The Western Infirmary was the nearest so I called a taxi and off we went.

I was worried she was going to die. She was living in Crathie Court at this point and the taxi took us down Byres Road where there's a pub called Wilsons. In the 80s, it was very well known. To my surprise, she asked the taxi to stop and got out. I thought perhaps she wanted to walk the rest of the way but nope she asked me to look inside and see if Terry, her partner, was there. He was easy to spot because he was 6ft 4in and always wore a seaman's cap. I told him I was taking Mum to the hospital and he said OK in his broad Irish accent. He wouldn't come out and just said he'd see her later. Mum, at that point, insisted on him coming out.

He appeared and said, "Well, Mary, what are you doing this time? Are you playing your games again?" I had no idea what he meant but she let rip.

"You big bastard, you!" she shouted. I was gob-smacked. She said she didn't want to go to the hospital and was ranting about Terry.

I managed to persuade her to let me take her home to her own flat and put her into bed.

"I'll be fine after a wee sleep," she said.

She was just about to close her eyes when a knock came on her door.

"Mary, are you in?" It was a familiar voice.

I was astonished when mum sat bolt upright and said, "Quick, that's Kathleen. Give me my handbag up." She took the bag from me and stuffed it under her pillow. She lay back down and pretended to be asleep.

I let Kathleen in and as I left I heard her wake mum. I had a smile on my face as I left. They seemed to be playing mind games with each other, I thought.

It was a weird memory to come to mind. I would be reminded of it many times over in the years to come. My fear of her dying, Kathleen stealing from her and the games they would play with each other.

To say in those first few days I existed on some surreal plane would be an understatement. We were just a normal Scottish family with all our troubles and strife like everyone has. We went about our daily lives in anonymity as most people do. We went to work, brought up our children, paid our bills and tried to enjoy life as best we could. Now my mother was front page news. It's not something that feels normal when a picture of your dead relative is staring back at you, happy and smiling, from the front page of a national newspaper.

To this day, whenever I see Mum's photo in the paper I feel sick. It's not something you become numb too. I was screaming inside: 'things like this don't happen to people like us!'

But it does and it did.

Her murder fed the newspapers for weeks. Seeing

headlines daily for a few weeks meant I never really got a chance to accept the circumstances of Mum's death. When someone you love dies in such a violent unexpected way grief hits differently.

With Dad we could be sad, hurt and angry, but you rationalise it in your head, dying is a natural part of living. You grieve and you move on. I was still in the disbelief stage of Dad's sudden death when Mum was ripped away from me. How do you come to terms with an unnatural death? I'm 70 now and I don't think I've come to terms with it ever.

Add into the equation that you don't have any answers, and you can perhaps understand a little of how I and my family were feeling. We were reeling.

I have a few regrets now. I wish I'd been more understanding of the trauma 24-year-old Martin Cullen went through finding his own mother like that. It must have been horrendous. Words to describe his feelings sound so cliche but how else do you express it?

I'm sure the hurt and damage endured by Martin is still with him today. I wouldn't wish that pain on anyone. I regret I didn't reach out to him at the time. I should have. Of course he might not have appreciated it, after all as siblings we were all very different people and didn't have much in common. But I should've tried. Hindsight is a wonderful thing, isn't it?

In those first few weeks I was consumed with my own

grief and slept fitfully. Mum was on my mind constantly. I felt as if I was stumbling through life at that point. I wanted to scream and cry and rail at the Gods for their cruelty. I didn't even know how she died so I would torture myself with awful thoughts. Why did she have to die? Who killed her and why? There was never any answer, of course.

There is a disconnect that happens when you're going through something so traumatic. I was aware everyone was talking about 'Wee Mary' and speculating who it was who had killed her and how. I also heard some police officers had taken the view that Mum was a woman of low morals who had taken a man back to her flat for sex and paid a hefty price. A prostitute in other words. Gone were the heady days of free love and peace from the 60s, now the '80s stood for conservatism and high standards. Single women who lived their lives were frowned upon. Kathleen was the one who told me that.

"Some of they polis think ma ma was a prossie. Fucking cheek of it. One of the cheeky bastards said she probably took a man back to her hoose. Ma wouldn't have done that," Kathleen told me. She was furious. She said she left the officer with a flea in his ear.

When I think about the attitudes of some of the police it still annoys me to this day.

It must be noted that not all of the murder team

thought like that and most of them treated my mum and our family with the utmost respect but, as always, in any large organisation, there are a few bad apples.

For a while after Mum's death, my home was used as a hub by the family to gather. I didn't mind, it kept me busy and my mind occupied. People would drop in and out, sometimes just for a cup of tea and sometimes just to be around people who were going through the same thing.

Kathleen kept me up to date on the police investigation. I'm assuming as the oldest children, her and John, were the first contact people for the police. Sometimes I would hear things from my other siblings but we were all grappling around for information which was in very short supply. Kathleen told me they had put an experienced officer in charge.

It was the first time I heard Detective Inspector Iain Wishart's name. By all accounts he was an excellent police officer who had been successful in a number of murder investigations and had worked on over 100. In 1984 there wasn't such a thing as a family liaison officer. If we wanted to know what was happening we had to chase up Strathclyde Police ourselves.

Committing a murder in the '80s was easy. Forensic science as we know it now was still a thing of the future. CCTV didn't come along until later in the decade with only a few private companies adopting it as a security measure, DNA blood profiling was in its infancy and wouldn't be used in a criminal case until 1986 down in England.

Two girls, Lynda Mann and Dawn Ashworth, were raped and murdered in the Leicestershire area in 1983 and 1986. Both crimes bore similarities and police suspected one man was responsible.

A man named Richard Buckland confessed to the murders but when they analysed his sperm samples, and the samples collected from the victims they didn't match. All men in a certain age range were asked to give a DNA sample and 4,000 men volunteered and were tested. But no-one matched.

Six months later, a man named Colin Pitchfork was overhead in a pub saying he sent someone else to the testing to evade analysis. The police did manage to get a sample from him, and it matched. Pitchfork was arrested in 1987 and sentenced to life in 1988.

It's ironic Pitchfork – the first man convicted using DNA – was released on parole in 2021, the same year my mum's killer went on trial.

But back in 1984, all of the progress made in forensic science around the world and down in England didn't mean anything to DCI Wishart and his team. All they had was fingerprinting and local knowledge.

In those early days of the investigation, we were hopeful police would find the killer quickly. Surely someone would know something and come forward or get full of the drink and slip up by saying something they shouldn't? However, the universe had other plans.

Quite often it would be a newspaper article rather than the police that would keep us up to date with what was happening.

One day there was a newspaper story where the reporter had spoken to her neighbour. Again, this was something new I learned about Mum – I had no idea she was 'friends' with her neighbour to such an extent he had a spare key for her flat.

Anthony De Marco told the newspaper he was surprised when he hadn't seen Mary for a few days. Usually he saw her every other day and they would stop for a chat or if they were just passing each other, a wave. He often popped into her flat for a chat. Mary was his neighbour but also she had become a friend, he said.

Although it wasn't unusual for Mary to vanish for days without any notice, she often went to visit one of her children without saying, this time felt different. It had made him feel uneasy. He'd told her many times to let him know when she was going but she never did.

Something felt wrong about it. The lights had stayed off for days, the curtains unmoved. And the silence from her flat had become impossible to ignore.

Clutching the mortice key Mary had once given him "just in case", he tried the door. Locked. Not just with the mortice, someone had turned the yale latch from the inside. But if Mary was away, who had locked the yale?

He'd felt dread but there was nothing he could do. He didn't have contact details for anyone.

The next day, the area was swarming with police. It didn't take him long to find out Mary had been found dead in her house. And rumours swirled that she had been murdered.

Once he learned of her death, he told a local news reporter: "Mary had a heart of gold."

And he said one thing confused him, the killer had taken the time to lock the door behind them.

Perhaps to delay discovery of her body?

More than 40 police officers were crawling the streets of Partick, knocking on doors, setting up a mobile incident room in the forecourt.

The word was out: someone had murdered Mary McLaughlin.

DCI Wishart took charge of the investigation, facing a wall of questions and a community living in fear.

No one knew how Mary had died, not yet. But it was clear to the public that it wasn't a natural death.

Police were staying tight-lipped – even with us, her family. But behind the scenes, officers were piecing together the fragments of Mum's last known movements.

Her partner Terence McLaughlin, a merchant

A CALLOUS KILLER

seaman, returned to Glasgow to a devastating welcome. The worst kind of homecoming anyone could receive.

At Partick Police Office, he was told the worst news. Mum was dead and her death was suspicious.

He cooperated with their inquiries, but there was little comfort to offer him. Nobody in the family knew anything and the police were keeping their cards close to their chest for the time being.

Terence 'Terry' McLaughlin wasn't my mothers husband, not legally, anyway. The newspapers at the time got that wrong, but then again, true facts often got bent in the rush to publish first.

Mum and Terry had never married. They couldn't. She was still legally married to my father, though their relationship had ended long before. Even so, she took Terry's surname, and from then on, Mary Mullen became Mary McLaughlin in everyone's eyes but the law.

Maybe the police told reporters she was married, thinking it lent her death or her life a certain respectability? In 1984, living with a man without being married was still frowned upon in certain quarters.

Or maybe the police simply didn't know at that time that she still carried her first husband's name on paper. It struck me on more than one occasion that I truly didn't know the minutiae of her life.

Regardless, that incorrect detail never sat right with

me. It was the first of many distortions about Mum to be made public.

I didn't know Terry all that well. He was around, but never central. Their relationship, like all my mum's relationships, was chaotic. Volatile. They met around 1969, shortly after she left John Cullen. A pattern was already forming back then, one she repeated again and again: she'd fall hopelessly in love, convinced this time was different, only to eventually walk away and start the cycle again.

Mum and Terry were together for about 15 years, though by 1984 things had grown uncertain. He was away at sea more often than not, he worked on the Oban to Mull ferry, and she had, as always, chosen to live alone. Independence was her shield, even when it left her wide open.

I only saw Terry a handful of times after Mum was killed. Grief seemed to hang off him. He moved into the Seaman's Mission near Whiteinch Close for a while, just across from the Clyde Tunnel. It didn't last. He drifted, first to Kathleens, then eventually to live with my sister Carol, where he stayed until he died five or six years ago.

I often wonder how deeply her murder cut into him. He must have blamed himself. If he hadn't been at sea, if he'd come home sooner would she still be alive? There's no way to know.

A CALLOUS KILLER

One thing has always stayed with me, though: the keys. The ones the killer used to lock her front door from the outside were never found. She only just had the locks changed, paranoid about her safety. For security, she said. The bitter irony of that still stings today. Some security.

10

The Hunters

FAMILY MEMBERS who knew mum's habits insisted she would never let anyone she didn't know into her flat, but she would welcome you if you said you knew her family. I remember once having to shout through the letterbox who I was before she would let me in even though it was daytime and she was expecting me. I found it inconceivable she would let her killer in unless she knew them, especially so late in the evening.

Had she disturbed a burglar? It was possible. Everyone knew she lived alone so anyone with a mind to could've taken it upon themselves to rob her house knowing that even if she was in, she would be no match for them.

The first seeds of suspicion had started to grow in my mind. Has someone she knew introduced her to the killer? Or, worse, was the killer someone in her own family? Once those thoughts took hold in my mind, I couldn't shake them.

Some things had gone missing from her flat – a plate with a rhyme my sister had bought her for Mother's Day was gone. It has never been found. I was baffled. Why take that? It was worthless.

The locked door bothered me, along with the missing keys. Logic tells me the missing keys and locked door were done to delay the detection of her body for as long as possible. Was the missing plate a coincidence? Had the killer taken it as some sort of sick memento?

So many different stories were circulating. Some of them were laughable if you can describe something so awful as that and others were just plain daft. One in particular made me laugh, when someone suggested Mary was killed by a hitman. What? Who on earth would pay someone to kill a wee 58-year-old granny from Glasgow? But that was the state of play – everyone was coming up with their own theories and suspicions and the family were all looking at each other warily and wondering 'was it you?'

How ridiculous it seems now. Perhaps if we'd been closer it wouldn't have been like that but we were a scattered family and there was a lot of ill feeling. Petty arguments would blow up into full scale fights and it could be over nothing at all.

When a detective came to see me about my statement

and what I could tell him about Mum, I remember saying to him that I thought the killer was someone known to Mum or her family.

He just shrugged and said, "Most women are killed by someone they know. We'll know soon enough." His confidence was high.

A dragnet was thrown around Partick. I would be walking to the shops and see detectives coming out of houses or closes having been round questioning people. I'd see people crossing the road to avoid talking to me but equally there were people who wouldn't have given me the time of day before stopping me in the street and asking about the investigation.

Some local women were understandably nervous. Most murders were domestic and it was clear Mum's was not. This made women fearful a serial killer was on the loose and men protective and gung-ho, ready for anything. We were told to make sure our doors were locked, not to walk the streets at night and not engage with strangers.

For weeks Mum's murder was the 'talk of the steamie' and people would be speculating and adding arms and legs to the story if they were unsure of the details. I can't describe to you the feeling when you're in the supermarket and someone wants to tell you the 'truth' about Wee Mary's murder.

The detectives pulled in as many local sex offenders

and criminals they could, they checked who was in prison and who was out and if their past crimes showed even a hint of trouble or violence towards women they were pulled in for questioning.

Everyone who gave an alibi was checked out and the neighbours were spoken to over and over until the police realised they had gleaned every bit of information they could. Family members were called in several times, people she drank with in the pubs, people she played dominos with, the local chip shop where she was last seen alive.

There were very few people in Partick who weren't spoken to at some point about Wee Mary.

The police were stumped. They had no motive, no suspect, no real understanding of what had happened to Mum in her final few hours of life.

As with everything in life though, things moved on quickly and Mum was being quietly forgotten and other events or local gossip were taking over. Fears began to dissipate and life was resuming normally in Partick once again.

Oh sure, it was a terrible thing that happened to Wee Mary but did you hear about Maggie leaving her husband for... I'm sure you get the gist of how it goes.

There can be no denying however the seventies and eighties in Scotland were a terrible time to be a woman. In fact, between the years of 1968 and 2004, there had been 1,000 murders of women across the country. A staggering loss of life, and many of those at the hands of the numerous serial killers who were operating in the UK during those two decades.

I know in the very early days of the murder investigation it was quickly ruled out that Mum had been the victim of one of those serial killers proving elusive to police. Some of those killers wouldn't be identified until the 1990s/2000s. Among the two most notorious was Angus Sinclair – nicknamed the World's End killer – who first killed a 16-year-old in 1961 in Glasgow before moving onto the east side of Scotland to the capital, Edinburgh where he abducted, raped and murdered two 17-year-old girls in 1977. He's believed to have carried out four other murders of women in Glasgow the same year, but detectives could never prove this. All of these young women had been on nights out. The search for their killer was, at the time, the biggest manhunt Scotland had ever seen. It would be 2014 before he was finally convicted of two murders and die in prison in 2019.

Robert Black, born in Grangemouth near Stirling, was convicted of the kidnap, rape and murder of four girls aged between five and 11 in a series of crimes committed between 1981 and 1986 in the United Kingdom.

It's strange to feel relieved when you're told, "No, she wasn't killed by a serial killer." As if the fact she'd suffered at the hands of a lone psycho as opposed to a spree-killing maniac made any difference to the reality of her brutal death.

It occurred to me that Mum had become another statistic. We didn't know then she'd be part of another unwanted club for over 30 years – the unsolved murder club.

It was a few days before details began to emerge about what had happened to Mum and the horrors that my brother Martin saw when he forced entry into her house. Kathleen did tell me Mum had been strangled because she said Martin had told her that but I thought to myself we don't actually know that because no death certificate had been issued and the police hadn't said. At that point I thought it was pure speculation. Even though Martin had been there and seen her, I thought perhaps she'd died another way and the police were keeping that quiet. When her death certificate was released a year later, I didn't want to look at it. I still haven't to this day.

We knew she'd been out on Wednesday 26 September with my sister Kathleen. She'd been in the Hyndland Bar, her usual pub, where she played dominoes and chatted with other punters.

Kathleen told the police she'd left earlier (than Mum) to get a bus home and that was the last time she saw Mum alive.

People from the pub said Mum was her "usual cheery wee self" and was in good spirits.

At about 10pm she left and walked along Dumbarton Road to Armando's chip shop. She bought a bag of fritters and a packet of cigarettes and left. A taxi driver saw her walking alone with her shoes in her hands. About 100 yards along the Crow Road, she was seen in the company of a much younger man.

It was the last time Mum was seen alive. Neighbours reported they hadn't seen her for a few days but that was nothing unusual so nobody thought anything of it.

Such was her habit of disappearing, the regulars in the pub didn't notice either.

The first real lead came nearly a week after Mum was found.

Detectives, combing through fragments of her last known movements, had finally managed to pin down a sighting.

Late on the night of Wednesday, September 26th, just after 11pm, she'd been seen walking along Crow Road, not far from her flat in Crathie Court. She wasn't alone.

A young man was with her. Tall, slim, clean-shaven. Someone described his hair as brown, neatly cut but bushy at the sides. Maybe a prominent nose. He wore a bomber-style jacket, possibly green or grey, with matching collar and cuffs, and the rest of his clothing was light.

The height difference between him and Mum would've stood out. She was tiny, barely over five feet. Whoever this man was, he towered over her. They'd been seen walking close together, in the direction of Laurel Street. Police now believed he might have gone home with her that night.

They never said outright that he was a suspect. Just that they were "anxious to trace him." That they needed to "eliminate him from their enquiries." But the implication was clear. This man was the last known person to see my mother alive.

Detectives flooded the area, knocking doors, repeating the same description to anyone who'd listen. Green bomber jacket. Slim build. Prominent nose. Did anyone see him? Did anyone know him?

But no one came forward. Not then. Not ever.

I couldn't even say out loud Mum had been murdered. It took a long time for me to be able to say that word. I didn't want to know the ins and outs, but it was difficult to avoid all the chatter within the family or in the newspapers.

I was only recently able to look at the crime scene photos. For some reason unknown to me they have been in the public domain for a long time. My poor Mum, dumped like rubbish. The pictures show her lying on her back wearing a green dress. There was a ligature around her neck, it was very long and had lots of knots in it. It was the belt from her dressing gown. She was never the best housekeeper, so I imagine her flat was probably in a bit of disarray for the police. It would've been challenging for them to determine the mess left behind by her killer and Mum's usual chaotic housekeeping.

I torture myself wondering about her final minutes on this earth. When did she know she was going to die? Did she suffer? Did she fight? Did she scream for help that wasn't coming? Did she try to charm her killer into backing off? What was her last thought? Was it regret or fear?

We found out Mum had been naked on her bed – which had been stripped of the sheets – when he strangled her. Then he put her dress on back to front. Was it panic that made him do that or some sick joke in which only he knew the punchline? Her beautiful new green coloured dress that she'd recently bought. I often wonder why she wore it that particular night.

The Hyndland Bar was what we called a 'spit and sawdust' pub, a working man's establishment where locals congregated, and everyone knew each other. It's still there today but it has a new name, the Partick Duck Club, and has probably been refitted many, many times since 1984.

Why did she choose that night to wear a new dress? She was only playing dominoes in her local pub. Did she have plans to meet someone? It's a question I can never have answered but one that haunts me. I remember asking Kathleen why one night and she just shrugged her shoulders and said nothing.

At what point did he decide he was going to kill her? From the moment he saw her on Dumbarton Road, or was it during their walk to her flat? Or over the cigarette they shared inside?

It pains me to think that the last thing she saw was his face, his ugly grotesque face as he revelled in her last moments, snuffing out her life. I hope she closed her eyes. I hope that somehow she found the strength to just close her eyes and not give him the satisfaction of terror his evilness desired.

We know that the scene of crime officers who attended had the presence of mind to bag every single piece of evidence they thought relevant in case it could be used. Fingerprinting was the only scientific method used by Strathclyde Police but every day I thank God those officers were savvy in thinking ahead and preserving the other pieces of evidence. I'm sure the killer didn't imagine for a second that a knot tied in Mum's dressing gown cord or a thrown away cigarette end would one day be his downfall.

Glasgow had a very unenviable reputation. At the time it was considered the murder capital of the world. Can you imagine? At the time Mum died, Edinburgh was in the grip of a heroin and AIDS epidemic and Glasgow homicides.

When people think of our beautiful country today you'd hope it's about our rich history, lochs, glens, mountains and the vibrant tapestry of culture and innovation with friendly people. But in the eighties, it was viewed as one of the most dangerous countries in the world to visit. We were considered more dangerous than America with its guns and Mexico with its drug gangs. What a way to be known to the world. There were murders in Glasgow every week it seemed. And killers were walking freely among us.

Modern murder investigations rely heavily on forensic science aided by good old fashioned detective work. In 1984, it was a boots on the ground and sheer luck approach. A wing and a prayer more like. That's not to say detectives didn't try.

DCI Wishart and his team worked hard on their investigation. What we know now is they were never going to solve the case, however hard they worked.

I never met DCI Wishart, it was mostly his boss, Detective Chief Superintendent Charles Craig, the family dealt with but from what we understood DCI Wishart was highly regarded. Especially when newspapers printed glowing articles about him leading the hunt for Mum's killer. They did a spread on all the major officers on the case and called them 'The Hunters'.

This gave the family confidence her killer would be found quickly.

Wishart had seen his share of violent crime, but I know now something about Mum's case cut deeper with him. Maybe it was the senselessness of it, or the way Mum had been killed without warning, without clear motive, without being shown any mercy.

Wishart wasn't the usual hard-nosed cop people might expect from Glasgow. A university graduate with a law degree and two decades of policing behind him, he understood the law not just as a tool but as a principle. He'd served years in the Partick division, and the hunt for Mum's killer had landed squarely in his hands.

He retraced her last known steps with clinical precision. He pinned down details you and I wouldn't think to consider.

Her familiar midweek routine. Her usual haunt, trading banter with the regulars. Her walk to Armando's cracking jokes with staff and asking, as always, for them to say goodnight in Italian. A running joke, that for her, never got old. Her bag of fritters. Her packet of cigarettes.

Wishart pinned down the sighting of the man seen with her. Not a neighbour, not a relative.

The contrast between Mum and the tall stranger beside her was striking. It should have stood out. It should have been memorable. And that's what frustrated Wishart most.

Despite the detailed description, the press attention, the man never came forward. And no one else could identify him.

Wishart didn't hold back his disappointment.

"The public response," he told the press, "has been underwhelming. It could have been much better."

He had a point. Hundreds of people moved through that area every night. Locals. Taxi drivers. Late-shift workers. Students. The Hyndland Bar was always busy midweek, and Dumbarton Road rarely slept. Someone must have seen something. Yet silence lingered. Nobody could offer anything.

Every Wednesday night since Mum was last seen, officers returned to the streets she had walked along. They retraced her route, speaking to anyone who passed by, hoping that a new face might jog a memory or that guilt might loosen a tongue.

It was barely a mile from the bar to her flat – a twelve-minute walk. But somewhere in that short distance, something catastrophic occurred. Mum met a murderer.

Detectives had taken more than 6,000 statements, mostly from people in the area. Between 45 and 60 officers worked the case at any given time, many of them volunteering to postpone their annual leave or cut holidays short to stay involved. Door-to-door inquiries.

Re-interviews. Endless hours were spent chasing a ghost.

The murder of Mary McLaughlin had clearly affected the force. They didn't want Mum to be just another statistic. She was known. She was loved. And yet, she had been silenced with brutal efficiency and now, it seemed to the police at the time, protected by a community unwilling, or unable, to speak.

And for those of us who loved her, who ached with the loss of her, that silence wasn't just frustrating. It was devastating.

We found the public's silence disheartening to put it mildly. Mum was so well-known around Partick, always stopping to chat to someone, always recognised, that it seemed impossible to believe no one had seen anything. In those early days, we clung to the hope that the answer lay close to home. That someone, somewhere, knew something and would eventually come forward.

How wrong we were.

As the weeks dragged into months, the energy around the investigation began to fade. Every day without a breakthrough felt like another nail in the coffin of justice for Mum. No new witnesses. No fresh leads. The hunt for the mysterious young man went cold. The promises we'd heard in the beginning, that everything possible would be done, started to sound hollow.

That is not to sound critical of Wishart and his team –

I know how hard they worked and how frustrated they were that their investigation had yielded nothing at all.

In February 1985, just a few short months after we lost her, Strathclyde Police made the decision to wind down the inquiry. Officially, they said no murder case is ever closed. Unofficially, we knew better. Resources were pulled. Officers were reassigned. Other murders needed attention. Other families needed their own questions answered.

The reality is, a murder investigation can only run for so long. In the beginning, it feels like the whole world has stopped to catch the person who destroyed your life. But as time goes on, and leads dry up, the world moves on. New tragedies happen. New grieving families appear. Officers are forced to chase fresher horrors, while older cases like Mum's are quietly placed on a shelf, gathering dust.

They call it a cold case. But for us – the family left behind – it is never cold. It burns, it haunts, it possesses every single day.

Many years later, Iain Wishart would give an interview to the *Daily Record* newspaper in which he said that Mum's case "haunted" him. He'd gone over and over it in his mind through the years wondering if there was something they missed during the original inquiry. Hundreds of people had been interviewed, fingerprints lifted from Mum's flat had been checked, alibis had been examined, the police ran reconstructions of Mum's final evening, they questioned local criminals relentlessly, especially sex offenders, family members were spoken to numerous times, neighbours were asked if they heard screaming or seen anyone running but there was nothing.

Mum was dead but her killer was the real ghost.

I remember the last conversation I had with DCS Craig when he came to tell me they were ending their investigation.

"Write everything down Gina. Whatever you hear, write it down and go to the police. Don't ever stop listening."

I had no idea then his words would be the catalyst for a 30-year-search for the truth. But I was determined about one thing. The only thing I could do: my mother would not become a forgotten victim.

11

Shame

I N NOVEMBER 1984, Mum's body was finally released by Strathclyde Police for burial. The family were told that due to the circumstances of her death, cremation was not an option. We agreed her funeral should be held in St Peter's Chapel in Hyndland Street. As I was the practicing Catholic in the family, I was tasked with making the arrangements for the chapel and her funeral mass.

Mum was raised a Roman Catholic and had her first Holy Communion and Confirmation at St Peter's and, like many of the women in the parish, she helped to clean the chapel too. It seemed fitting that this should be the place where her final farewell would take place.

I had been baptised in the nearby St Simon's in Patrick Bridge Street. Confusingly, St Simon's was the original St Peter's. The first mass there was by Father Daniel

SHAME

Gallagher in 1858. That same Father Gallagher taught the great African explorer David Livingstone Latin which enabled him to qualify for medicine at Glasgow University. But by 1903 a population surge meant a new chapel was needed so the new St Peter's Church was built on the Hyndland Street site.

I visited the parish priest to make the arrangements for the receiving of her body and the mass. He took the details and said he would call me back later.

The next day I was shocked when he called to say he did not know my mum, and from the information he had, she was not a practicing Catholic. It was unlikely her funeral could be held there but he would need to speak to the Monsignor.

The following morning, I went back to the chapel where the housekeeper showed me into a room that was lavishly decorated with red velvet winged armchairs. Isn't it funny the details imprinted onto your mind when you're actually in great distress? It wasn't normal for a Monsignor to be involved with funeral arrangements, so it felt strange sitting there – as if I was waiting for some kind of divine judgement to be passed down. I wasn't far off the mark.

The door opened and the Monsignor himself glided into the room. He was cold and unwelcoming. The atmosphere was tense. He paced up and down, refusing to make eye contact.

"I understand your mother has died and that you want her funeral service to be held here?"

"Yes," I replied.

His response shocked me.

"I now know who your mother was and the lifestyle that she lived. She is not in the catchment area for this church. I cannot give my permission for her funeral service to go from here."

His words were racing around in my head. 'The lifestyle she lived. The lifestyle she lived. The lifestyle she lived' – I couldn't stop saying it to myself as I comprehended what he was saying.

I knew there had been vicious rumours in the early days after her murder that my mother was a 'Scarlet woman' who liked the company of men. There were hints and jibes that she was a prostitute. Nudge nudge, wink wink. As if she was somehow deserving of the end that had befallen her due to her lifestyle.

These rumours were untrue. Even as early as last year someone said to me about her being a sex worker. Many years ago I would rush to say no, she wasn't, but my view now is even if she was, so what? Did that mean it was a justified murder?

Back in the chapel, a supposed 'Man of God' was standing before me telling me a woman who had been murdered was not 'worthy' enough to be given a funeral by his church. How dare he condemn my mother.

To this day, I do not know where the courage to stand up to him came from, but I was furious.

"Who are you to judge my mother? In our faith, or any faith for that matter, God is the only judge, and it's God's judgement who comes to us all on Judgement Day."

My words had no impact as he replied very coldly and dismissively, "I can see that you are upset, but that is my decision." He turned on his heels and walked out.

Shaking and near tears, I slumped down on the chair and let the anger give way to sorrow. No dignity at the end of her life and no dignity in death. I wanted to rail at God. How could he let this happen? She didn't deserve this. Was I going to have to go round chapels and beg for my mother to be allowed a funeral in the religion she practiced and believed in? Or was it going to be a service in a church who didn't care who came through their door? What could I tell my family? This would cause ructions and more angst. We were all on edge as it was. The shame!

I stood up and was just about to leave when the Monsignor returned. I eyed him warily.

There was still no compassion in his eyes or grace in his voice as he declared he would allow Mum's funeral to take place in St Peter's.

I don't know what happened when he left the room. Perhaps the housekeeper had appealed to his better nature? Perhaps he said a prayer and felt God had given him permission? Who knows? I just remember feeling nothing but relief.

I nodded my thanks and left before he could change his mind again.

The police said Mum's casket would have to be closed due to the length of time since she'd died. It meant none of us would be able to see her to say a last farewell. The usual tradition was the coffin would be open and mourners would be allowed to kiss the deceased's head. Under no circumstances can the coffin be opened, said the police.

Her body was taken to Kathleen's house the night before the funeral. This was far from ideal as it was a one-bedroom flat with a narrow hall. The undertakers had to carry the coffin up three flights of stairs and manoeuvre it around some very difficult angles to get it inside the flat. First they reversed it into the kitchen. There was a thud. Someone let out a gasp.

"Oh God, what was that?"

I was horrified. The sound was obvious. Mum's body had slipped down inside the coffin and was bumping against the wood. I can still hear that 'thud' in my mind to this day.

I remember feeling annoyed. All of this could've been done from the funeral parlour. Mum had suffered enough in life, was she meant to suffer further indignities in death too?

A police officer was present – in case someone became hysterical and tried to open the coffin. There was a lot of sadness that we couldn't see her for one last time. Someone actually said, "How do we know if it is really our ma in there?"

As was customary, we sat around her coffin and chatted. My great aunt Lottie was there. It had been years since I saw her last. As a child I was afraid of her, she was a battleaxe and could have a cruel tongue. She was short, plump with a loud voice and a bossy nature. To me she was intimidating but clearly the terror she had instilled in me as a child was not something that she regretted or even remembered.

"Which one are you then?" she said in her derogatory tone.

My memory flashed back to childhood and the way she made me feel. It was no different to now even as a wife and mother myself.

"Gina," I replied.

"Well, what's this I've been hearing that you had a row with the priest about having your ma buried from St Peter's? You had no right to badmouth your mother and try and stop her funeral." she shouted at the top of her voice.

I was so distressed all I could do was run from the room. Lottie was still a bully.

Kathleen came into the kitchen behind me and asked

what the fuss was about. I told her and she went back and explained to my aunt, but this made no difference. There was no apology for getting it wrong, it would seem.

I made sure I left Kathleen's flat soon after. I found it all so energy sapping and I needed my strength for the coming days.

The morning of her funeral dawned. It was a dull cloudy day. I didn't mind – it suited my mood.

It was heartening to see so many people lining the streets for mum as her funeral cortege made its way to the chapel. So many people turned out for Mum that day. The Partick community had come out for one of their own – Wee Mary. She would've liked that. I like to imagine she was sitting in heaven chuckling away as was customary, even during so sombre an occasion.

It was a fitting service for Mum, religious and dignified as she deserved. Her final resting place is in Maryhill Cemetery, just 500m from my dad's grave. She is buried beside John Cullen who died in 1992 and her son Brian. Michael, her oldest child is buried in a grave back to back with Mum. The irony is not lost on me that despite being separated for 29 years in death my parents are closer to each other than they were in life.

I felt sorry for my big sister, Carol, who still didn't know her dad was dead and her mum had been murdered.

SHAME

She was away at sea with her husband who was an engineer for a shipping company. I had managed to get a message to the company he worked for but it was a few weeks before Carol was given the horrendous news. By the time she was able to get home, the funerals were over.

It did feel nice, if that's even an appropriate word, that at least Mum's funeral was something normal we could do for her.

The police officers who gathered to pay their respects and watch the crowd for signs a killer was in their midst was a startling reminder that this was no ordinary funeral and no ordinary death.

Once her funeral was over a lot of squabbles broke out over who should have the property belonging to Dad. I didn't pay any attention to it. For me the most important thing was to focus on Mum's murder investigation.

12

A Whole Lot of Speculation

VERY EARLY into their investigation, the police received a 'confession' from someone claiming to have killed Mum. They had been called to Woodilee Hospital in Lenzie, East Dumbartonshire. The hospital was originally called an asylum and had first opened in 1875. I was surprised when a police officer called me to tell me what had happened.

My youngest sister, Marie, never called Mary "mum" or "ma". It was always "that woman".

Marie had suffered with mental health issues for a long time and was in and out of Woodilee, which actually closed its doors for good in 2000, when she called them and said she had "done it". Two officers duly went to interview her, and Marie told me this is what happened.

She said she knew who had killed her mother and

what the murder weapon was. Remember at this point, the police didn't know us, the family history, the dynamics or drama so they felt at last they were getting somewhere. But their hopes of a swift conclusion were shattered when they interviewed Marie.

The detective asked her, "Who did it then?"

"Me," she replied.

"What with?"

"I took a gun and shot her."

The detectives looked at each other and not discreetly shook their heads in disappointment. While it was known Mum had been murdered, a cause of death or the weapon used had not been disclosed to the public. The police believed this needed to be kept secret because it was knowledge only the murderer would have.

"Right, thanks for that information, Marie."

They knew it had been a wasted visit, but they had to follow up all and any leads they received. Marie's claim was one of many about what happened to Mum.

I couldn't feel anything but sympathy with my baby sister. She had no memory of Mum at all until she went into Woodilee. Which isn't surprising since Mum left when she was just weeks old and as Marie grew older, she refused to have anything to do with her.

I remember having to look after Marie as a child myself and she was a popular little girl at school. She was the class joker but was easily led into trouble. Looking back now I think it was clear things weren't right for Marie mentally but she coped well. She was a fast runner and won lots of races for the school athletics team.

The police had taken over 600 statements from people. They were getting nowhere. Their investigation was drying up. Nobody came forward to identify the man in the photo-fit seen following Mum. He was a complete mystery. There had been no new information for weeks – it seemed to us as a family that someone was going to get away with murder.

There was a lot of chatter amongst the family, old arguments being rehashed, resentments bubbling to the surface, everyone looking at each other as possible suspects. Kathleen, who was always with mum, seemed to spend a lot of time with the police. No sooner would she get back from the Marine police office than they would be back at the door to take her down again. The familiar sight of a police car coming to get her began to rattle on nerves. Quite often it happened when she was at my house.

When I asked her about it, she said it was to go over her statement and would change the subject.

This made sense to me because she was on a lot of medication and seemed very confused at times. I wondered if she had made up tales during a drug-induced haze and now the police suspected her.

The alcohol and drugs distorted her memory, and she

would blame her sleepless nights for lapses in her concentration.

I started to wonder about my sister and where she was the night Mum died. Everyone knew her and Mum went out a lot together and she had confirmed she was with Mum the night she died.

More than a few minds were focused on Kathleen and whether she was telling the truth or not.

Word had been going round the family – and to the police – that in the lead up to her murder, Mum had a few disagreements with people including some of her own children.

Kathleen told me about one argument she witnessed when her and Mum had been in Mullin's Pub on the corner of Dumbarton Road and Mansfield Street. Kathleen said she heard her mum arguing with someone on the pub phone before slamming the phone down.

When she asked Mum what was going on, Mum said one of her son's was causing his "usual shit". Kathleen thought nothing more of it as the two of them had had rows before and always made up.

There had been a few incidents when Kathleen had to step in to stop it becoming physical. She told me once Mum had been in a fight with someone and the person had punched her causing her nose to bleed.

She said to me, "You know my ma, she winds people

up, a few people have wanted to punch her; she could start a fight in an empty hoose.

"Maybe her murderer was someone she had a fight wi' and they've left her bleeding. Ma ma bleeds easy and hemorrhages easy, so maybe the person went away and left her."

Kathleen made her sound argumentative and aggressive. A long-forgotten memory came to me. Mum was living in a flat near the art gallery, it was Christmas, and I think I was around six years old.

There was a pretty Christmas tree in the corner with real chocolate ornaments on it. They were wrapped in brightly covered foil paper and instantly I wanted one. Chocolate was a rare treat when I was a child.

Mum was out of the room so I ate it as quickly as I could and hid the foil evidence in my pocket.

She didn't say anything at the time but knew I had taken it and eaten it without asking.

She knew I felt ashamed and that was punishment enough as far as she was concerned.

Kathleen and some of my other siblings may have seen another side to my mum but I preferred to remember her kindness and good humour.

I often wonder why Kathleen would bring up stuff like that because by then we knew Mum had been strangled. Years later, I would mention this conversation to one of the cold case team but they said it didn't fit with the information they had. Meaning Mum's cause of death was nothing to do with bleeding or fighting.

I thought back to the last time I saw her alive – outside my dad's house when he died – and she had looked so sad, so sorrowful, that I realised that the jaunty, happy-go-lucky woman people got to see really was wearing a fake smile.

There was some chatter around the fact mum had worn a brand new dress she had bought to go to the pub that night. Why, I wondered, would she wear her lovely new fancy dress to a 'spit and sawdust' pub to play dominoes?

I asked Kathleen if she was meeting someone that night? A date, perhaps? Kathleen said she didn't know, she wasn't her mother's keeper, but there was something in the way she answered that made me think. She was defensive at my innocent question.

We knew from the police that Mum was alone as she walked along Dumbarton Road to the chip shop. She was known to the owners and they remembered that particular night because she was 3p short for her fritters. She'd been walking barefoot and carrying her shoes in her hand.

I remember asking Kathleen if she'd seen Mum that night and she denied it. The story would change again later, of course, and Kathleen would say she'd become confused over the dates.

"Stop asking me questions, Gina. I get enough of that from the polis. I don't know what happened to my ma!"

To this day, it still doesn't make sense to me why a random stranger would follow my mum home and she would allow them into her house. How did they leave? Not one person came forward during any of the inquiries to say they'd seen a strange man leave the flats.

Years later, one of my grandchildren, who lived in Crathie Court area, told me he used to play with friends in the 'back green' of the court and they would use a 'secret' entry at the bin area and play Tap Door Run with his pals.

I went back after he told me this and yes, despite living there myself and not knowing, there was indeed a door at the back. It had been boarded up when I visited in 2021. There is also a perimeter wall around Crathie Court that was built after 1984. I racked my brains trying to remember the layout when Mum died. It's entirely possible her killer was able to leave this way without seeing anyone.

But my stirring suspicions about my sister grew. I didn't believe her explanations and excuses. Her stubborn refusal to answer questions. Why were the police taking her to the station so often?

She was hiding something and I was determined to find out what it was.

13

Kathleen

WE ALL suffered due to our upbringing in our own way.

Kathleen was my oldest sister and my parents' first daughter so she was named after her granny who had died young. She spent much of her childhood being 'mother' to her younger siblings. I think she grew up feeling bitter and 'hard done by' having to shoulder so much responsibility for children when she was just a child herself really.

Despite the fact she was forced to be 'mother' because her own mother had abandoned her family, Kathleen was perhaps the closest to my mum and they spent a lot of time together as adults.

History has a way of repeating itself in many situations and Kathleen was following a path in life I didn't understand nor approve of. She left school at 15 and managed to get a job in Beattie's Biscuit Factory in Drumchapel. I remember when Friday afternoon came, the factory closed early and I would eagerly wait for her to bring home a big bag of broken biscuits, which could not be sold in the shops. It was such a treat as my father never earned enough to buy luxuries such as biscuits. Kathleen would then have to hand over most of her earnings to my father to help support the running of the home. She had very little of her hard-earned cash for herself.

When she was 17, she met Joe Boyle and fell in love with him. They got married soon after and went on to have three children: Elaine, Christopher and Gerald.

When her marriage to Joe was breaking down, she abandoned her children. They were very young at the time, and I think she just couldn't cope being a single mum.

Over the years I saw her do some terrible things, but I still kept in touch with her. Blood truly is thicker than water and I felt a pull towards my sisters even if we were all completely different people. Kathleen and I seemed to get on just fine, by that I mean we didn't have fights like she did with my other siblings.

If she was in an aggravated state, I would just leave and not see her for a few weeks. I found it helped to put distance between us for a little while. I'm not an aggressive person, I like to live peacefully.

KATHLEEN

Of course, I heard things about her — I always say there's no smoke without fire and in Kathleen's case, the world was burning. I always knew what she was capable of and when I asked why she behaved the way she did, I would be met with an angry outburst so I stopped asking and I suppose you could say, I turned a blind eye.

I had never really been one for listening to gossip but since my mother's death I had become suspicious of everyone and started listening more to what was being said around me. It's fair to say at this point we were all suspicious of each other. It was a soul-destroying, destructive time.

Even my own children would question why I had anything to do with Kathleen, but I tried not to be judgemental and went by my own experiences. She had never done any harm to me and so I decided to keep in contact with her.

She would tell me many stories about her childhood, some of them outlandish and shocking.

For instance, there was one that sticks in my memory.

Like many children, Kathleen remembered her first day at school. She went to the same primary as Mary did — St Peter's in Partick — which was run by the local nuns. Kathleen had a milk allergy but the teacher, Sister Mary Charles, would insist she drank it. My sister would protest and cry saying it made her sick but her tears would be in vain as she was forced to drink it. She would shake Kathleen violently by the shoulders and tell her she was ungrateful.

"Think of all the poor children all over the world who are going hungry with not even a drop of water to drink and here you are, child, refusing free milk!"

A distressed Kathleen drank the milk and that evening she was violently sick and unwell. Mum asked what she had eaten in school, so she said she'd been made to drink milk.

The next morning, Mary took Kathleen, her brother and the other two children, who were in their pram, to school. She held on tightly to Kathleen and waited as the lines of children went in before going to Sister Mary Charles' classroom. The class were saying their morning prayer when Mum knocked on the door.

As she left the class, she told them, "Best behaviour, don't forget God is watching you all, he can hear and see everything, do you all understand me?"

Mum didn't beat about the bush. She confronted the nun over the milk. The Sister lied and said she wasn't aware Kathleen was allergic.

"That is a lie, Kathleen told me she did tell you that it would make her sick, but you insisted she drink it."

Mary Charles was unrepentant. "In future, if there is anything your child cannot take, simply write her a note to give to me."

KATHLEEN

Angry at her attitude and in the heat of the moment, mum pulled off the nun's coif straight from her head! Kathleen remembered the horrified look on Sister Mary Charles' face.

Mum marched off satisfied she had made her point.

Kathleen was never forced to drink the milk again.

When I think about it now, who knows if Kathleen was telling the truth, but I never did see her drink milk at any time in her life.

Kathleen lived her life in total chaos. Some of it I witnessed, some told to me by others and some I learned much later in life. Some of it was quite shocking to me but a lot of it I had known about or suspected for many years. She was convicted of benefit fraud, shoplifting, supplying drugs, stealing from her friends and of course, we think she stole from my dad while he lay dead or dying.

While I witnessed her bad behaviour with others, I decided while she was living peace was the better option. Sisters falling out is probably very common. I expect it's nothing unusual in families – friends one minute, full blown enemies the next. We all knew what Kathleen was like and she would often fight with my other sisters. I found myself becoming immune to the stories I would be told about her.

Whenever I came back to Glasgow I would visit her wherever she was living at the time. In her younger days she liked to go out to the pub but as she got older she preferred to stay in at night drinking at home. Like my mum, everyone in the area knew Kathleen.

During one visit back home, I had arranged to meet her and my sister Patricia. At that time, Patricia was running the catering side of a pub so we organised a visit to coincide with when she finished her shift. It was early evening, the pub was busy, the karaoke crowd were just starting and everyone was merry and enjoying themselves.

After a few drinks, Kathleen and Patricia started to niggle at each other. I was sitting with my back to the wall facing Kathleen while Patricia was at my side.

Their sniping began to get a bit more heated and I just remember moving my head from side to side listening to them both thinking it was time for me to leave. But before I got the chance to stand up and leave, it reached boiling point.

Patricia had accused Kathleen of something which caused Kathleen to yell and point her finger in Patricia's face. Patricia warned Kathleen to get her finger out of her face but this was ignored with both of them getting angrier and angrier.

Patricia, who was sitting down, said, "I am fucking warning you, get your finger out my face or I'm going to fucking punch you."

Kathleen, who was standing up, lifted her fists up and

shouted, "Come on, if you think you're man enough to take me on!"

I remember thinking, "Jesus, I'm only here for a holiday," as Patricia again warned Kathleen to back off but Kathleen wasn't interested in calming down and started shouting, "Come on then" to which Patricia duly obliged and threw a punch at Kathleen.

Kathleen staggered back a bit, misjudged her chair and fell back onto the floor star-shaped, her glasses lying half over her nose. Some punters in the pub came running over and asked my sister if she was alright. She didn't respond, she just lay there while a man berated Patricia saying, "Imagine hitting an old woman like that!"

They said they could not believe what they were seeing. I told them they were sisters who often have fallouts and this seemed to appease him. The manager came over and asked Patricia to leave even though it wasn't actually her fault. Kathleen had deliberately thrown herself back onto the floor to make the incident look worse than it actually was. That was just one of the many scenarios that I witnessed over the years.

In 2019, her son, Christopher died. Christopher's life had been blighted by addiction, and it was a long cruel illness that took him way before his time. Kathleen told me she felt nothing but relief due to how he lived and his mental state while alive. She said she'd long hoped that he would die before her.

But she didn't shed many tears, and I couldn't help but think about how she had fuelled his drug habit by supplying him with prescription drugs including tramadol, dihydrocodeine and Valium. This was always done on the days his benefit money was paid even if he was in hospital she would visit or get one of her 'friends' to drop the drugs off.

Elaine, Kathleen's daughter, knew what was happening between her mother and brother and felt powerless to do anything about it. She did get an appointment with her mum's GP to say she felt the prescription was being abused but the doctor said he wasn't the police and couldn't do anything. She then tried her brother's hospital team and again came up against a brick wall.

I was a patient at the same practice so managed to have a word with my own doctor who discreetly changed Kathleen's prescription to weekly which would make it harder to sell on the drugs. Kathleen was furious and would call the surgery many times to get it changed back to monthly.

On the eve of Christopher's funeral, the plan was Elaine, who had only been reunited with her mum in 2011, was going to stay at Kathleen's. That didn't happen.

Elaine called me distressed. Her mum was drinking and their conversation got heated. There was an iron sitting on the kitchen worktop. Kathleen threatened to smash it across Elaine's head. Elaine left and came to stay with me.

We met Kathleen at the funeral home, and she behaved as though nothing had happened. The thought occurred to me that maybe she had mental health problems because to think she was just a bad bastard was too horrible to contemplate.

Kathleen suffered from poor health and a lot of it was down to her lifestyle choices, I suspect. She was quite often in hospital and then sent home again, the doctors unable to find anything wrong with her.

I was with her at one visit to a consultant who said after many tests and scans they couldn't find anything. Kathleen was a big woman who would bemoan the fact she was very overweight and would cry asking why she was so big when she rarely ate.

Elaine and I would share a smile at that because we knew it wasn't unusual for Kathleen to wake in the middle of the night and make herself a plate of mince and potatoes and wash it down with a can of Guinness. This was a regular occurrence.

So when she started to lose a lot of weight and her appetite we were alarmed. She went to see her GP who was so shocked at the weight loss she immediately sent her to the Queen Elizabeth hospital for tests.

After a lot of examinations she was told she needed

an ileostomy as she had a blockage in her colon. She also developed a hernia and needed more surgery.

In 2022 she was told she had colon cancer and refused to take any treatment as she did not want to lose her quality of life. As her physical health was deteriorating, her mind was still razor sharp.

Elaine and I made the decision not to abandon her. There is no escaping death, it comes to us all. Although she did some inhumane things to people, I refused to abandon her at her time of need. She kept pushing us away but there was nobody left in the family who wanted to keep in touch with her or help her.

We began to notice a pattern to her hospitalisations. She would go in for a few weeks, save her money and then when she was discharged she would go home feeling flush with cash and back to her habits of smoking heavily and drinking. And a lot of the time she was in hospital was when the cold case team said they were coming to visit her. She just didn't want to engage or answer their questions.

It was difficult to tell when she was faking and quite often she would give the nursing staff a hard time barking out orders. Then she would brighten up and say she felt fine.

For the next two years she ran rings around me and Elaine. So many times she would cry wolf saying she felt so unwell, we would drop everything and once in hospital she would be happy again. At times, Elaine could not help her mother due to the abuse and aggression she would heap onto her daughter. I would have to take over.

In an effort to offer her some comfort in her last days I took some things from her home, a soft tartan throw that smelled of her washing powder, some pictures of my dad, my mum, her two grandchildren, Emma and Lee, and a wedding picture of her and Joe. As I placed them on the window ledge of her room where she could see them from her bed, the film 'The Sixth Sense' came into my mind – the scene where the little boy from the film tells Bruce Willis "I see dead people". I couldn't help but laugh to myself. Not unkindly but more out of nervousness as I knew the end was drawing near.

I took her in food she liked and Elaine would do the same. We were just trying to make her last days comfortable. Not once did she say thanks to us.

I started to read aloud stories from a book written by the famous Glasgow comedian Stanely Baxter called 'Let's Parliamo Glasgow Again – Merrorapattur!' Which was full of daft stories meant to raise a smile.

"Oh shut up Gina," she said.

It took me all of my willpower not to say 'you shut up, you ungrateful bastard', but I kept doing what I was doing as I knew the time was coming when she would be silent forever.

I asked her, "Why do you treat us so badly when all we've been to you is kind?"

She was angry – even as her body was dying, she mustered up enough aggression to scream back at me. "What have I done for you? I have done plenty for you. I will tell you what I did for you? I brought you up, that's what I did." Her face was twisted with anger and venom spitting out her mouth.

I told her she was venting her anger, and it was OK but not OK how she was treating people.

She closed her eyes as if to sleep and refused to speak.

Two days later, on May 10 2024, I held her hand as she took her last breath.

I felt annoyed and cheated. There was some relief too because her quality of life had been terrible. But mostly I was overcome with a deep regret and annoyance because I had believed and still believe to this day that Kathleen knew something in connection with my mum's murder.

I'd, perhaps naively, hoped that on the road to meet her maker, Kathleen would feel guilt and shame and confess what we'd all long suspected.

I said to Elaine, "Well, anything she knew, she has taken to her grave, as I always suspected she would."

Why would I do it? Why would I bother to be so devoted to someone who had seen it as their right to behave the way they did? It wasn't just because she was

KATHLEEN

old and ill because that was the way she behaved her whole life. I did it because it felt like the right thing to do. I wouldn't leave a dog to die alone.

As she lay on her deathbed I had the opportunity to ask her if she knew who killed our mother before she took her last breath and I did think about doing it but to me it felt morally wrong. Besides, stuff like that is what happens in movies, it's not real life.

A few months before she passed, Kathleen had taken great delight in telling me, "My ma always used to say trying to get information out of me was like trying to get blood out of a stone." She was proud as punch at that.

On the night my mum was last seen alive, there's a missing two hours where Kathleen asked Christopher to give her an alibi and lie to the police. During the original investigation in 1984, one of the police officers came to my home.

He asked me, "Which of your sisters was pregnant in 1970?"

I had to think for a minute before I replied but told him I was pregnant in 1970 and my sister Carol had also given birth in October 1970. I couldn't remember if Margaret was pregnant, but I said I would ask her.

He told me the reason he was asking was because during their inquiry, they had discovered that Mum and one of her daughters were sharing a boyfriend. I felt physically sick at this revelation and couldn't comprehend it. I spoke to Margaret after he left and told her what he'd said.

She said it wasn't just me and Carol who'd been expecting but also Kathleen who'd given birth to her son, Gerald, in July 1970. By this time, Kathleen had split with Joe and was living in various addresses. Her children were with their dad.

How could I have forgotten about Gerald? Everyone in the family had speculated about his birth as Kathleen and Joe had split when she became pregnant. I'd looked after him for a while when Kathleen asked me to babysit when he was three months old so she could go for a night out and she never came back for him.

He'd become unwell and I had to take him to hospital. The hospital informed the social work department who couldn't trace her either. I offered to look after him, but they said I was too young and inexperienced even though I was pregnant myself with my first child.

Gerald was eventually taken into care and adopted legally. It makes me sad when I think about him but on the positive side he was spared all this family's heartache. Elaine did try to find her brother about eight years ago but she couldn't get any information as his name had been changed and it was a closed adoption. She has searched adoption and family reunion sites and left her details in the hope he would see it and get in touch.

KATHLEEN

Elaine is happy for me to share that information. But perhaps his new parents have never told him and he is in blissful ignorance of his start in life. Personally, I hope wherever he is, he's had a happy, healthy and peaceful life.

The bombshell from the police was completely impossible to understand. How on earth could anyone have a relationship with a mother and daughter at the same time? Would my mum have even done such a thing? I refused to believe it.

As immoral as it was I had to ask them what bearing did it have on Mum's murder? It was 14 years before she died even if it was true. I felt they were clutching at straws. It wasn't something you could just forget or ignore, I mean if the police were asking about it maybe it had some significance to Mum's murder?

I did confront Kathleen about it and she denied it. She said the police were liars and just trying to stir up trouble for her. She was known to them, she said and it was easy for them to try and pin the blame on her. In 1984, I accepted her explanation even if I couldn't quite get to grips with it but after Christopher told me in 1991 about his mum forcing him to lie my suspicions about Kathleen began to take root.

Why did she ask Christopher to lie about her whereabouts? Did she know Mum's killer? Had she introduced him to Mum? Was she in the flat when Mum died?

Did she kill Mum? Did she turn a blind eye while Mum was being strangled to death?

Was Mum killed by one of her own children or were they shielding a killer?

14

And The World Keeps Spinning

THEY CLOSED the book on Mum's murder very early in 1985. Officers had been re-assigned onto other cases, the leads had long since dried up. The police were baffled. They had no murderer or motive and they couldn't continue indefinitely. My greatest fear was coming true: while my mum was lying in the ground dead long before her time, her killer was living his life as free as a bird.

The police said the case would never really be closed but the reality was unless someone or the killer came forward, her case would never progress. Nobody gave a thought to what the future might hold in terms of forensic science.

I don't think in 1985 I even knew that those words existed and, for us, the technology we take for granted today, was like something out of a science fiction movie. I remember saying to an officer, "As far as I'm concerned, someone in my family killed my mother."

His reply was a shrug and "we'll never know".

I felt downcast and heavy.

1984 was a momentous year in history. Among many notable events that year we had Ronald Reagan – a former Hollywood superstar – re-elected President of the United States, Indira Ghandi was assassinated, Sally Ride became the first woman in space. The British miners went on a strike that would last a full year, the first Apple Mac Computer went on sale, Policewoman Yvonne Fletcher was shot outside the Libyan Embassy in London, we first learned about the dreadful famine in Ethiopia and Band Aid was formed.

But for me, I always describe it as my 'annus horribilis'.

Who can forget our late Queen Elizabeth using that very term in 1992 to describe the year which saw Prince Charles and Princess Diana separate, Windsor Castle go up in flames, Princess Anne divorce and Andrew and Sarah York split.

When I heard the Queen's speech on television and she said that, I remember thinking to myself, "At least you have the money to restore your castle and the people you speak of are still alive whereas my horrible year has left me with two dead parents and an unsolved murder."

What could I do but try to move on with my life?

That first Christmas without Mum and Dad was horrendous. She'd only been dead a few weeks but we tried for the sake of the children to make it somewhat merry and festive while inside I just wanted to curl up into a little ball and disappear inside myself.

We went to midnight mass on Christmas Eve and I just sobbed the whole way through the service to the point people were giving me side eyes and feeling uncomfortable. The family wanted to congregate at my house but I said no, it didn't feel right so soon after both of them died. I'd never gone a Christmas Day without seeing my dad and I couldn't help but reminisce over previous years. It was slightly different with Mum. We never got presents from her that I remember but Dad would go to the famous Barras market on Christmas Eve if he had money and get something for us all.

Sometimes the welfare people in John Street would bring a box of donated toys. One year a new neighbour had moved in and she had a little girl, Francesca. The mum, Frances, was in a wheelchair and I felt sorry for them, especially the wee girl because she never came out to play, she would just stand at the window watching us all in the street. I took my only present from the welfare people and knocked on her door, thinking she was poor like us.

Her lovely mum invited me in to play with Francesca

and said I was so kind to bring a toy. When we went into her bedroom she had a room full of toys. It taught me to never judge a book by its cover.

Spring 1985 brought a rare flicker of light into what had been a long, heavy winter for our family.

I had just moved into a new house, a semi-detached place with a small garden, nothing fancy but it was mine. After everything we had been through, having a new space felt like a new beginning, or at least the possibility of one.

That May, my sister Patricia was getting married to her fiancé, George Stack. It was a moment we all needed, something good to focus on, something to celebrate. When Patricia told me they hadn't settled on a venue for the reception, I didn't hesitate. I offered them my house. It wasn't grand, but it seemed right to start their new life in a home that already held so much hope for ours.

On the morning of the wedding, my house buzzed with a rare kind of excitement. The air was filled with the smell of hairspray and perfume and the nervous laughter that always seems to hang around big days. I helped Patricia with her hair, carefully fixing each strand into place, trying to steady my hands and quiet my heart. When she slipped into her outfit I had to catch my breath. She looked absolutely stunning.

For a few precious hours, the dark cloud that had

hung over us for so long lifted. There was music, chatter, the clinking of glasses, and for once, real laughter. I remember standing in the doorway of my living room, watching Patricia make her grand entrance, and feeling an ache I couldn't push aside.

We all thought the same thing but hardly dared to say it aloud: how we wished Mum could have been there to see her. I could almost picture Mum clapping her hands together in delight, her face lit up with pride.

But it was Patricia's day, and none of us wanted to drown it in sadness. We kept the memories to ourselves, celebrating as best we could, knowing she would have wanted that for her, for all of us.

Despite the happiness and the sense of normality the day seemed to bring, the truth was never far away. Tragedy had touched our family once already, and deep down, I think we all sensed it wasn't finished with us yet.

As is often the way with big families, there was always someone, or something, stirring up a bit of drama. With so many of us scattered between different homes, different lives, it sometimes felt like there was a constant background hum of problems waiting to erupt. Some were small, the everyday kinds of disagreements that come and go. Others were far more serious.

And then there was Brian.

My half-sibling Brian's life was short and not without trouble. Brian had a twin brother, David, who did all his communicating for him. Although they were not identical twins, David just seemed to know what Brian wanted to say. It felt like they were the same person in two bodies.

Brian had always been withdrawn, even as a child. He would simply point to anything he wanted and David would fetch it. He didn't make any effort to speak even though he could.

It caused problems at school with his learning. He would refuse to answer questions from teachers and would sit with his head bowed.

In the months after Patricia's wedding, just as we were beginning to think we might be pulling ourselves back together, tragedy found its way to our door again – this time, through Brian.

As a child, he'd been angry and disruptive and once set fire to a school. Social work became involved and Brian was sent to a child psychologist. It was later recommended that he be detained in a unit for disturbed children. It was never determined what caused this.

By the time he was 18, he was living as normal a life as was possible for him.

He was an exceptionally handsome young man. Approximately 6ft tall, thin and pale and with brown hair. He had a girlfriend and seemed to be getting his life together. The only fly in the ointment was he couldn't get a job.

He would occasionally visit me and tell me how down he was feeling and that no-one understood him. He felt he'd been let down by his father and mother. Brian felt abandoned as we all did. He felt very strongly that due to his past behaviour no-one wanted to know him. His sister, Patricia, was close to him but she was getting married and had her own life to live as she should've been.

His girlfriend, Sharon, was his strength. Sometimes she would visit me or call and she told me she did love Brian but she found him hard work, especially his temper and mood swings.

It was discovered that Brian was addicted to gambling machines and would spend all his money on them. Sharon, who suffered from depression herself, said it was too much for her. Brian needed to get a job and curb his gambling addiction. So he tried for a few weeks and it was working well but one day he went to sign on at the dole and collect Sharon's prescription and didn't return home.

Sharon and David became concerned and contacted police who said they were not worried as he had signed on for work with the social security office. They told the family he probably wanted to be alone for a while.

Two weeks later he was still missing. They checked again with the employment office but he hadn't signed on which meant he had no money.

Four weeks later, a man taking a shortcut home noticed a heap of clothing lying in the grass. On taking a closer look he realised it was a dead body. It was Brian.

It was established that Brian had taken a short cut via the canal on his way home from picking up Sharon's prescription. The grass on the bank of the canal was very high so when he slipped and fell, his body was hidden by the long grass. The procurator fiscal's report determined he had overdosed on Amitriptyline, which was Sharon's. Their verdict was accidental overdose and hypothermia.

The theory was he'd collected his benefits and succumbed to the temptation to gamble and lost all his money. Unable to face the consequences knowing it would kill his relationship, he took her medication to help him cope with what was to come. They surmised that he had overdosed by accident.

The shortcut Brian used was a popular route. Anyone passing would've assumed it was rags discarded. After his body was found, my sister Patricia and one of my brothers went to visit the area where Brian had died. There they saw a carpet of green, yellow, black and brown slime where his body had lay.

The area was swarming with maggots and flies. What was left of his hair that had detached from his scalp was lying on the grass. The smell was pungent. Patricia promptly threw up the contents of her stomach. They took a lock of their brother's hair with them and were in a state of distress, the council had not cleaned up the area. One of Brian's brothers later returned to the area, doused it in petrol and set fire to it.

Just four years after his mother's murder Brian died aged 22. I feel nothing but sadness when I think of that time. Brian didn't deserve to die like that, his siblings did not deserve more heartache. The spectre of death and destruction was still feeding off my family. How much was one family meant to take?

After Mum's funeral, my husband and I decided we would try to make our marriage work. I had my doubts, I didn't want any more alcohol-fuelled violence and I knew deep down I was very unhappy but for the sake of my children I had to try.

I was also aware on some level that I was scared of being alone. I had never been with anyone but my husband and I had a deep-rooted fear of abandonment and loneliness. A gift from my parents.

So we bought a new house in March 1985. We thought a new environment and new surroundings would plaster over the cracks in our relationship. Such immature thinking but I didn't know any better.

At first it felt like we were in our honeymoon period again, everything was wonderful. The affection had sparked back into life and we were talking to each other more. He tried to reduce his alcohol intake but we had many get-togethers especially on his side due to the sheer size of his family.

He had five brothers and I had my three sisters who I kept in touch with. From my husband's side, we had 22 nieces and nephews alone. Which meant there was always a reason to celebrate something – a special birthday, an engagement, a birth, a Holy Communion or a Confirmation.

While they were really good times as his family were lovely, I realised I was actually drinking more than I should have been to keep up with my husband. I thought by joining him it would save my marriage but it began to go downhill again. The abuse restarted, mostly fuelled by alcohol on both sides. I was, like my mother before me, using alcohol as a crutch and an escape to this situation I found myself in.

I knew he was never going to stop and me joining him wasn't the answer. We were hurtling towards early graves and leaving our children orphans. The thought filled me with horror. There was nothing more important to me than my children. I felt powerless at first. I didn't know where to go or who to turn to. There wasn't much help for women in my situation. Safe houses and refuges were just taking off. If they'd existed before I wasn't aware of them.

One night we had a massive fight, fists were flying, the

house was rattling with anger, both of us seething with resentment. It was bedlam.

My oldest daughter hit me with a lightning bolt: you need to divorce. My children had seen and heard enough and Laura wasn't scared to say it. The reality of how bad things had become hit me, this was it. It was time to leave my marriage.

I longed for my mother, like with most difficult times in life, I so wanted her to be there. Despite being desperate to keep a family unit together for my children, I realised I was actually doing more harm than good. The decisions I made had to be in their best interests. I needed to be brave and strong and cast away any doubts I had about supporting my children or where to begin picking up the pieces of my shattered life.

We agreed to divorce. It was hard for both of us. Despite the violence, deep down there was some love there but that is not enough reason to stay in a toxic relationship that is harming everyone. If I learned anything from Mum and Dad's sudden deaths, it was that you only die once but live every day.

As an aside, today I have a good relationship with my ex-husband. He's a great dad and once our marriage ended he changed his ways. Sometimes you have to lose everything you love to change and that's what he did. Alcohol brought out his demons and he knew that.

I have nothing but a deep respect for him despite our marital issues.

The children and I stayed in Gairbraid Court until it was sold and then I moved to a temporary address in Summerston, Glasgow. My oldest daughter went to stay with her dad. We still kept in contact with each other.

To support myself and the children I was doing shifts with social work home support and took a part-time job in a nightclub on the weekends. The children would stay with their dad but if not my oldest daughter would look after the two youngest. Life was moving fast.

15

A Breath of Fresh Air

O N A night out with my friends, not long after I split from my husband , I got chatting to a handsome young man eight years my junior. We discovered we both came from Partick. He'd never been married, was charming and had a good job. He had no excess baggage and no children.

I was naive and probably very immature. Still bruised from my marriage disintegrating, I found myself being caught up in the heady early days of romance where everything is nice and lovely and they shower you with affection. I believe the modern term, according to my grandchildren, is 'love bombing' which is regarded as a red flag in relationships today. I wish someone would've shown me a red flag when I met him. It might have saved me a lot of heartache.

I was reeling from his attention and giddy with excitement. I couldn't believe this gorgeous young man was interested in a divorcee with three children. It didn't take me long to realise I had jumped from the frying pan into the fire.

Of course I married him almost as soon as the ink was dry on my divorce papers. By this time my daughters were living with their partners so it was only my son living with me when my new boyfriend moved in.

We eventually bought a house in Glasgow's salubrious West End. An area noted, even today, for its affluence and trendy bars, shops and expensive houses. It was 1990. Glasgow was moving on from an industrial city to one that was named European City of Culture and the city transitioned well to its new status. It was showcasing itself to the wider world and we felt as if we were living right at the heart of it in the West End.

I was working as a GP receptionist with the Greater Glasgow health board. I decided to set up a community care business while still working full-time.

The marriage ended as abruptly as it started. I came home one day from a doctor's appointment to find he'd cleared the house of any trace of him. His wardrobe and drawers were empty. He'd left me.

I was heartbroken. I'd never been on my own but I vowed there and then I wouldn't be dependent on anyone ever again. Emotionally or financially.

I seemed to always be dealing with problems of some

sort — I felt so alone. It reminded me of mum and how alone she was. You can be in a room full of people and still feel lonely. My dad had always said to me when I was growing up that I should never allow anyone to take my dignity from me.

In 1995, I moved house again to a new flat with my son. My care business was going from strength to strength. Deciding to keep my flat in Glasgow, I moved to Troon, Ayrshire to live by the sea. It felt good to put some distance between myself and the city where I only knew heartache. In Troon, I wasn't murdered Mary McLaughlin's daughter. I was just 'Gina'.

I was free from seeing ghosts on every corner. At last I felt like I could breathe again. I needed to forget the bereavements, the pain, the suffering, the nightmares of Mum's murder and Dad's sudden death. I needed to live my life. Fate had other ideas.

By 2002, with a thriving care business and after school club I felt it was time to move onto other things in life. I completed a University degree, I finished a course on teaching English as a foreign language and a business course, but I was restless.

My mother was always at the back of my mind. The feeling that she was with me was strong. I had put one foot in front of the other since her death and I had coped well with whatever life was throwing at me. I was aware I had chances she did not. I acknowledged the hardships she had endured throughout her life and used her strength as a crutch for my own whenever I was being challenged.

I had long since stopped looking at every stranger's face in the street thinking "was it you?" However, it was always there in my mind stalking me. Chipping away. I had been taking notes of everything that seemed relevant since 1985 and occasionally I would re-read them as if the answer to the questions were suddenly going to leap off the page and hit me in the face.

I was suspicious of everyone in the family who had contact with Mum. Whenever I was back in Glasgow, I wandered down to the Hyndland Bar when I felt strong and would chat to the locals who knew my mum in the hope they would tell me something they didn't tell the police.

I could be having a conversation about the weather and would find a way to bring Mum into it.

I wasn't a police officer, my detective skills were non-existent but I was intelligent and I had an almost photographic memory where I could recall chunks of conversations and details so insignificant it would drive me crazy.

I regularly turned up to the police station to ask what was happening with Mum's case. More often than not I never got past the front counter where a bored desk officer would take my name and details and assure me someone would be in touch but in all honesty nobody ever did.

It was draining me. It felt like nobody was caring. Not even those charged with keeping the public safe. Many times when I would say, 'I'm here about the Mary McLaughlin murder' the officer behind the glass would reply, 'who?' and I had an urge to scream, "A mother of 11 who was brutally murdered in her own home and you lot have let a killer go free!"

Of course I didn't, I would sigh, smile out of politeness and be on my way, bereft yet again. Feeling helpless. Scotland was suffocating me. I thought by escaping to Troon I'd have some respite but this wasn't the case. My children were grown up and had their own lives to lead. I decided to move abroad.

Türkiye appealed to me after a holiday there with my friends years before. I chose to spend nine months of the year living there and three months back here in Scotland.

I lived in an old Turkish village, far from the crowds and package holidays in Marmaris.

I managed to get a job teaching English as a Foreign Language in a kindergarten in Antalya. I loved it but over the years I would teach in Mersin and Konya too.

The peace and tranquility was just what my racing mind needed. The history and the culture quietened my demons… well, almost.

It was in Türkiye I met my husband, IIyas. He is 16 years my junior and this year we will celebrate 15 years of marriage. We had planned to spend most of our lives living in his village but after seven years of commuting back and forth to Scotland, my health started to decline.

I was 58 years old, it was time to go home.

I needed to sort out my impending retirement and due to my health – high blood pressure, high cholesterol, pre-diabetes – I was reminded that I wasn't a teenager anymore.

I planned to sort out my health and work until my expected retirement age of 60. It was around this time that the government moved the goal posts and raised the retirement age for women to 65. I missed the cut-off date for women who were born up until March 31st 1954. My birthday was June 1954.

I'm what's known as a WASPI woman (Women Against State Pension Inequality). This was set up in 2015 after 3.8 million women were hit with an extra five years of work with little to no notice from the Government. I lost out big time on being able to retire and this change in pension age had a big impact on my life. Faced with working for another five years but also needing to fix my health issues, IIyas and I knew it meant leaving Türkiye.

We decided he would stay in his own country while I returned to Scotland to sort out my affairs.

At first I stayed with a relative but after a few months it was no longer suitable for me. I found myself homeless again. My children would've offered me a home in a heartbeat, but I did not want to impose on them. They had their own lives. My choices were limited.

Houses were in short supply but I attended a meeting at the council homeless unit and told them my story. While I waited to be offered somewhere, I sofa surfed with friends and family.

Due to my increasingly fragile health I was offered a home within six months. But, like mostly everything in my life, it didn't come without a shock.

The flat I was offered was in the same building that my mum died in some 30 years previous. I was the same age she was when she was murdered. I was in disbelief and staggered.

If I didn't accept it, I'd be going back down to the bottom of the housing queue. It made me feel sick to my stomach. I tried to explain to the council but their hands were tied. There were limited houses for rent.

I felt very unwell, unsettled and had to fight the demons in my head about taking the flat. This meant I would see, every day, the house where my mum was murdered.

At the end of the day, I had no choice. I felt the council were being cruel but I was stuck. I accepted their offer with a view to exchanging as soon as possible.

The flat was at the opposite end of the building to where Mum lived. I made sure never to use the entrance she would have. I refused to look up at her window, I just couldn't. Then something strange happened.

One day I just felt overwhelming acceptance. Not peace – anyone who has lost a relative to murder most likely will never know peace again – but a belief that, spiritually, I was placed there for a reason.

I felt that Mum was watching over me and urging me to never give up searching for her killer.

Since the day she died, Mum was never far from my mind. It was time to rake up the not so distant past.

16

Diamonds and Pearls

MY MIND was troubled on a regular basis. I took to singing, in my head, a line from a Beatles song called 'Let it Be'.

I would see Mum's face and ask her what she would do. Did she want me to continue for the whole truth or to let it be?

Did I want to stir up a hornets nest by going over the past?

There were some relatives who weren't happy with any meddling and wanted it left to the police but, despite leading a busy life, I couldn't rest, couldn't let it be. I felt Mum was haunting me, urging me on.

Could I take the stress I would be putting myself under? Was I putting myself in danger?

What if the killer heard and decided to come for me too?

For years I had kept things written down. Suspicions I had. Snippets of conversations I had heard over the years. The police investigations had long since dried up. *The file is still open* was their mantra. *We need new information to come to light.*

But nobody was looking. Not that we were aware of anyway. I later learned that between 1985 and 2019 there were four reviews of Mum's file by various detectives who hoped to solve it.

I'm guessing by the fact that we were rarely contacted the reviews did not even get as far as examining statements from those of us still alive.

I decided it was time to get the story of what happened to Mary Ann McLaughlin out there.

I wanted, no, needed to fight her corner. From the day she was born, nobody had fought for Mary. I did not want her to become just another statistic even though she already was – a murder victim, an unsolved cold case. I couldn't allow her murder file to be gathering dust on a shelf and forgotten about.

There were times the police would claim no knowledge of her existence let alone her murder.

There are dozens of unrecorded visits I made to the police with information. Unless I'd rocked up with the killer in tow and evidence into the bargain, they weren't interested in the ramblings of a middle aged woman regardless of the fact her mother had been murdered.

She was my mother and without her, myself, my children, grandchildren and great-grandchildren would not be here. I may have muddled my way through my own life, but I was blessed. I had my family and they loved me. I knew if anything had happened to me, they would do the same as I was doing for Mary. I was confident enough, relentless perhaps, in my determination that nobody would forget the name Mary Ann McLaughlin.

I began to write Mum's story. The words flowed as I wrote everything down. I decided to self-publish a fictional book based on Mum. I needed people to know about her. It wasn't much but it was the best I could do.

Every morning I got up at 6.30am and walked the square mile of Partick with flyers which carried the synopsis of my book. I posted them through every letter box I could until they were done. Mum had lived and died in that area.

I thought if any answers were coming, it would be from someone reading the book and coming forward with information. I planned the launch for December 2013.

I came under criticism for 'exploiting' Mum to make money. I want to make it clear here and now I did not cash in on my mum's murder. In fact I lost a lot of my own money with the book. Friends left my business cards, with the book details, on planes, buses, trains, subways and bus stops. Anywhere, really.

I donated copies to Save the Children charity shop in Byres Road and was delighted when they sold out in days. Mum would've been pleased with that too.

My book, like this one, was a labour of love and a tribute to my mum. But, alas, like the police, nothing was forthcoming. Nobody knew anything about her death.

The police, however, did come to see me. They wanted to know how many copies had been sold and about the people in it. They wanted to know who was fictional and who was real. They were wanting to go over statements from 1984 and were particularly interested in Kathleen's rent cheque deception. As with many visits from the police, nothing ever came of it.

The book, which was a form of therapy for me, was absolutely useless in terms of solving her murder. However, I did feel that in some small way, I'd been able to share her story with a small number of people.

I withdrew it from publication many years ago. I felt it had done what I needed it to do. It had soothed my mind and made me more determined to find out what happened to her.

At last it was time to leave Crathie Court. I was able to exchange my flat with someone else.

On the day I left I found the courage to look at the window of my mum's flat. I was filled with a mixture of emotions: sadness at all Mary had lost and missed out on, regrets about our relationship and the chance we were denied.

But I felt hopeful because it was 2016 and a turning point had come. An article was published in the *Daily Record* by their crime reporter, Jane Hamilton.

17

The Weight of Alibis

JANE HAMILTON knocked on my door one day in early 2016.

She said she was doing a series on unsolved murders and wanted to include my mum's story.

There hadn't been any interest in the story for a number of years, not in any real depth anyway.

I had a deep distrust of the media since articles had appeared previously with words from me by journalists I hadn't spoken to. But Jane had the courtesy of asking me if she could feature my mum's story in her series. She said she did not like families opening up the paper and seeing their dead relatives' faces staring back at them.

I liked her approach and I had a sense that she was genuine and was not trying to do Mum's story just for headline-grabbing attention. I sensed she was a good journalist and when I did my research I could see she was a crime writer with many years of experience. I agreed to meet her at my flat.

Jane and I spoke for several hours, she asked lots of questions and at the end she said she would keep me updated. Although I liked her instantly, I took her words with a pinch of salt as my dealings with the media had not been positive so far. But she stuck to her promise and kept in touch with me.

Jane is a kind, empathic soul who instantly understood the impact my mother's death had on me. She wanted to get the story right and wanted to tell it in a meaningful way. She tracked down Iain Wishart and managed to speak to him too.

I am convinced that the article Jane wrote about my mum highlighted the case again for police and forensics for the first time in many years. Jane's work brought to light other important factors that would become clearer in their relevance to my mum's case.

UNSOLVED DAY THREE OF EXCLUSIVE SERIES ON CASES THAT SHOCKED SCOTLAND

Jane Hamilton Crime Reporter
Daily Record, Tuesday March 1, 2016.

Unsolved: Retired senior detective and victim's daughter tell how they are still troubled by Mary Ann McLaughlin's murder case 32 years on

FORMER Chief Superintendent Iain Wishart said he is still baffled by the murder and describes Mary Ann McLaughlin's case as "the one that got away".

IAIN WISHART had a long and distinguished police career.

But despite rising to the rank of Chief Superintendent in the former Strathclyde Police, Iain often thinks about the only case he couldn't solve as a detective.

Mary Ann McLaughlin's murder is, he said, "the one that got away".

Mary, 58, had been found dead in her Partick flat on October 2, 1984. She had been strangled and her body had lain for six days before a concerned relative forced their way into the building in Crathie Court.

Iain, who retired in 1998 after 35 years in the police, said: "It was a baffling case at the time and has remained so to this day. Mary Ann's murder is the only one I didn't solve.

"I was senior investigating officer for around 25 years and worked on about 100 murders in total. The big question then and now was who would want to murder Wee Mary?"

The mum of 11 was last seen alive on Wednesday, September 26, when she left the Hyndland Bar and walked along Dumbarton Road to the local chip shop, Armandos, and bought cigarettes and a bag of fritters.

Iain said: "Mary was in a good mood that night and was laughing and joking with staff. She would always ask them to say goodnight to her in Italian.

"About 100 yards from the chip shop she was seen in the company of a young man and they walked the Crow Road. Frustratingly, we never traced that young man and it was the last time Mary was seen alive.

"I remember it being a difficult inquiry. We didn't have forensics back then and I had a suspect very early on but after questioning him many times I knew he didn't do it.

"There wasn't any help from the locals either. We were disappointed in the lack of response. The area was busy at the time but not one person came forward."

Iain said that three days after her body was found, Mary's bra was discovered in the back garden of the tenement flat.

He added: "It wasn't 100 per cent conclusive it was hers but Mary's boyfriend at the time thought it might have been. We didn't even know if there was any significance to the find as there was no evidence of a sexual assault but it frustrated me then that the area wasn't searched completely. Policing back then was very different to modern methods."

The 71-year-old added: "Her case touched many officers

who postponed holidays or returned early from annual leave to help with the inquiry.

"We took hundreds of statements but eventually, without any further evidence to go on, the investigation was scaled back. About 10 years ago, myself and my deputy at the time were asked to go in and review the files with a cold case team but they didn't seem to get anywhere either.

"I'm certain the answer to Mary's murder lies locally."

Just as the murder has troubled Iain, Mary's daughter Gina McGavin is so tormented by it she has vowed to never stop looking for answers.

Gina struggled so much to come to terms with the brutality of her mother's final moments she wrote a book in a bid to try to move on.

She said: "People write crime books all the time but I lived it so I felt able to write about it with some authority.

"The book, Diamonds and Pearls, was never intended to be a big seller or make me money. I wrote it as a way of keeping my mother's memory alive."

Gina, now a 61-year-old grandmother, was grieving her father's death when Mary was murdered just weeks later.

She said: "My dad, Joe Mullen, brought me and my five brothers and sisters up after he and my mum split up. I was just two then. I wasn't as close to her as I'd have liked. She was a poor soul but not a bad person.

"I'm convinced that whoever killed her knew her. She wouldn't have let a stranger into her house. I just hope that one day we can find out who and why."

This view is shared by Iain Wishart, who said: "Mary would talk to anyone but I think whoever killed her was known to her. It would be closure for her family if this case could be solved now."

****

On the day this article ran, fate would have it that one of my daughters, Gail, worked in Glasgow University. She was working in the forensics department and as she was going about her work, she realised all of the scientists, working in different rooms, each had a copy of the newspaper open at Mum's story. She decided to be bold and asked one of them if there was the ability to extract DNA from a case, say, 30 years ago?

Yes, came the reply. Technology had moved on and in Scotland they were making great strides in DNA analysis.

"The reason I'm asking," Gail said, "is that picture you are all looking at, she's my gran."

One of the scientists asked if her own mum was still alive.

Yes, she told them.

"Tell your mum to go to the police again and ask them to look at your gran's case," the scientist said. "Ask them about the latest DNA technology. I cannot request it, but your mum can."

When my daughter relayed this to me, it was all the encouragement I needed.

I practically ran to Partick police station armed with a copy of The *Daily Record* and asked about my mum's case. I was told someone would look at it and be in touch.

There is no record of me having visited the station that day which saddens me. Nobody was in touch and again I was left hanging, thinking no-one cared any longer about the murder of an old woman 30 years before.

We now know Police Scotland had begun another review of the case but they had not informed the family of this. I still firmly believe Jane's story reminded them they had the evidence in storage from Mum's house. Nothing will change my mind on that.

We know it took a long time for the science to catch up but I believe the article in the *Daily Record* changed everything.

While there might have been work going on behind the scenes with the police, on a personal level, there was a family problem. My nephew, Christopher, then aged 49, came to visit me around that time. He would come periodically over the years. Especially when he was distressed. I was the 'go-to aunt'.

Christopher was a good looking man, about 5ft 5in tall with a fair complexion, slim built with a good head of hair he always kept tidy. He was a gentle person, kind and softly spoken. He was troubled and needed to vent.

Christopher repeated allegations to me he had previously said in 1991 and 1992. His story had not changed or deviated in all that time. He said his Mum Kathleen had lied to the police and everyone about the night his granny, my mum, died.

By then I was keeping a diary. The following is an extract from that visit.

Friday June 24th, 2016

Christopher visited me last night around 6:00 p.m. just as I was going to go to the shop. He was in quite a state, asked to borrow £10 as electricity on the prepayment meter had run out. I said no, but I could give him some food. I asked him if he wanted me to call his mum but the answer was a very swift no. They'd had another fight – their second in a week. This is common because their relationship is volatile and toxic at times. He left almost as quickly as he arrived. I tossed and turned all night because I was worried about him so I decided to visit him today out of concern for his welfare. He looks so poorly. We chatted about family relationships and how volatile some of them had been over the years and the impact it was having on Christopher's mental health. He agreed and said he would go with me to get help. He then told me his mother, my sister Kathleen, had stolen £20-25 from the bank and had since got a new bank card. He claims Kathleen knows something about my mum's death. When I asked him what he meant, he said she called the police when they were fighting and had them remove Christopher from the house. He shouted in anger that he wanted to make a statement. When the police asked him what about, he said it was about his gran's murder and that he had been covering for his mother for years. He said he thinks the police were dismissive of him because Kathleen was drunk. I told him that if he had information relating to his gran's murder then he should speak to the police. It could be important. He said he is sure his mum knows something and I could see he wanted to tell me more so I sat and waited. Eventually he admitted his mum had asked him to lie about the time she got home on the night my mum was last seen alive. Christopher said she didn't get home until 1am but told him to tell the police she was in the house by 11pm. I reminded him he had told me this story in 1991 and 1992 and had retracted it. He looked sheepish as he said he had been covering for his mum so pretended he was lying. I do not know what to do about this information.

Christopher's words were going around and around in my head. I didn't know what to do for the best. I checked with a legal friend who said there was no point in me reporting it to the police as it was hearsay but Christopher could go to them and make a statement saying his mum lied about her whereabouts on the night of my mother's death.

I knew Christopher would probably not do that. As much as his relationship with Kathleen was toxic, he was still torn with loyalties to her.

Two weeks later he turned up at my house again.

<u>Friday July 8th, 2016</u>

Christopher came to visit me again today at about 5.30pm. He had been at his mum's but left because he was feeling stressed. He repeated his claims about his mum asking him to lie and said he'd forgotten he'd told me many years ago. He said it was a Wednesday night his mum asked him to lie. The week before mum was found dead. I asked him why he was saying it all again and he said it was because of a fight with his mum a few weeks ago that it had all come back.

All I could suggest was he tell the police and let them decide if it was important or not.

He said the police would not believe him because he is a drug addict. Christopher said he'd told the police years ago and they asked him why he was saying such things.

I told him I wasn't there so I couldn't go to the police but it is something he must do for himself. I said it wasn't about me or his mum or even him but about justice for his gran who deserved it no matter how she lived her life or what she did when she was alive.

He said he would think about it and told me he'd lied for her several times. I showed him The *Daily Record* article from March and we discussed his gran's next door neighbour, his mum's then partner and someone else who was close to the family. Christopher said it was maybe an accident and the police had ruled out a lot of people years before. He hadn't seen the paper and did not know the case was being looked at again.

I suddenly remembered Kathleen's suggestion that someone might have left Mum injured and not realised she was dying. When he was leaving, I said to him inside, you are a decent person, if there is a time to go to the police, it is now. I said if you think your mum knows something, the police should be told.

He said he needed to think about what to do. He was a good person and I know he is troubled and caught up in a vicious cycle. I do want to push him. It's widely known his mum feeds his drug habit by selling him valium and that has contributed to how he is now.

She has a hold on him because of the drugs so if she asked him to lie what could he have done? All I can do is be patient. I have impressed upon him the need to do the right thing, I would support him. I do not know if I can keep this in and say nothing to my sister.

I closed my diary and slept another fitful sleep filled with dreams and nightmares of my mum and sister. This was driving me crazy.

It was clearly troubling Christopher. I spoke to my husband about it and he suggested I go visit my nephew again.

July 9th, 2016

I popped up to see Christopher today. I want to get him medical help or take him to Turning Point charity so he can get help. He has agreed to Turning Point. He mentioned his gran's murder again. He voiced his concerns that his mum was involved. He said she didn't have any marks or cuts on her and perhaps her and Mum had just been arguing. I have told him not to worry about it just now as my main concern is getting him well again. I have contacted Turning Point, but an automated email came back with a number. Christopher's contact person at Turning Point is on holiday.

After this entry, I didn't see him again for over a month. I had been to his flat many times but he was either not in or just ignoring me. I suspected he was feeling guilty for mentioning his theory about his mum's involvement in the murder. They were probably talking again, I remember thinking. Christopher would come back to me when they next fell out but as the weeks went on without any contact, my concern grew. I decided to try his house again.

Tuesday August 16th, 2016

I went to see Christopher about taking him to West Street for Turning Point. He told me he had visited his mum on Sunday and she told him to 'fuck off' and would not let him in. She called while I was there and asked him to come back. Christopher said he hated her and was going to the police to tell them about the missing two hours that he was asked to lie about. He said his mum's partner threatened to beat him up in 1984 if he told the police the truth. But he is dead now, I said. I told him he needed to forget about it all for a while and get help. I feel sorry for him. He showed me some out-of-date food his mum had brought him. His life is really sad. I will take him to Turning Point tomorrow.

Wednesday August 20th, 2016

Christopher wasn't home. I guess he doesn't want to get help at the moment. I have to put his comment out of my head for the sake of my own sanity.

Sunday 20th November 2016

My niece, Elaine, told me, out of the blue, today that Christopher has told her he lied to police. He told his sister he thought he was being asked to lie due to claiming rent for the flat he was meant to be living in when Mum died when Kathleen cut in and started shouting and yelling at him telling him to stop living in the past. Elaine was annoyed. She said her mum never lets her and Christopher talk. Kathleen threw Christopher out again while Elaine was there. The flat they were renting when Mum died was mine. It came out during the murder investigation that they were still claiming rent from the benefits office and hadn't told them they'd left. Elaine told me Kathleen would go round on the day the cheque was being delivered and stop the postman. She would tell him she would take the mail to her son and would then cash the cheque. I don't know how long that went on for but I was furious with her. I'd had to sign a form saying I had not rented the flat nor received rent from Christopher for a specific period after he left. I am confused how he would think lying about his mum's timings was something to do with that scam.

It was months before I saw Christopher again. This was a bit unusual but it wasn't entirely out of the ordinary. Since 1985 the family had fractured. Everyone was getting on with their own lives and trying to move on. Even though mum had abandoned us all, it would appear she was also the tentative piece of string that helped keep her children together so when she died, the string snapped.

Wednesday 5th of April 2017

My door buzzer kept going off. It was 6.30pm. I was in the backroom of the house and just ignored it. I've had a dreadful day and I'm always getting buzzed for the neighbour's parcels, the cleaning service and anyone else. You'd think I'm the only person living here. A few seconds later I heard Christopher shouting up at the window 'thanks a lot Gina'. I ignored it. He's probably wanting money again. I've been thinking about it a lot. Kathleen always says Christopher gets mixed up easily about things, she's been saying that for years. I don't believe it. I don't know how many times she's changed the story on those missing two hours. Christopher wasn't on drugs at that point as he was very young and had just begun to dabble. Kathleen insists she got the bus at 11.10pm that night and Christopher wasn't home. She said she went out to look for him at 12.40am but she forgets that I remember everything. She told me a few weeks ago that Christopher had come home 'full of it' and she'd taken him for a walk at 12.40am to walk it off. Christopher keeps saying his mum has got away with it. He remembers a lot more than she thinks.

Thursday 6th April 2017

Another fraught day. Christopher came here again at 2.30 p.m. asking if I would go to his mum's for his TV and electric meter key. He told me about his fight with her yesterday and I told him I did not want to get involved.

My head is bursting with it all. I told him about last night and shouting up at my window. I wasn't pleased at all. He had the grace to look sheepish. Anyway, I went to his mum's but I made him phone her to tell her I was coming to collect his things. Kathleen was OK when I got there and a neighbour helped with moving the stuff to my car. Christopher ranted all about the things his mum did, he called her a whore and said she was selling drugs. He shouted he was going to tell the police. He is angry. She said she is not going to collect his medication on Saturday. I told him he can do that for himself. I dropped him off but at 7.45pm he was shouting up at my window again and pushing my buzzer. I ignored it so he buzzed a neighbour who let him in. He was shouting through my letter box. I have no idea what about as I stuck my fingers in my ears and refused to listen. He left after 15 minutes. I am drained with it all.

Friday 7th of April 2017

Elaine and I went to see Christopher. He said he went to the police last night and gave a statement. They're coming to see him again but he needs to go down to Stewart Street station. He said she thinks she's 70 and got away with it but she has not. I am glad my niece was with me. He was going on about fights with his mum and having to lie for her. Christopher said he fought with Kathleen about lying and she said she would pass a lie detector test if made to take one. He told her to get one done.

It was five months before I heard from Christopher again. He had gone back to stay with his mum. I learned from my daughter that he had told her the same things years before. It became apparent he had made the same accusations to a number of people. What stuck in my mind, and still does, is how his story never changed in all those years. If it was made up, why would he be so insistent all these years later that his mum had secrets about Mary's murder?

Friday September 8th, 2017

Kathleen seemed a lot brighter today. She had a copy of a Sunday Mail *article from last week on her shelf. She brought up the subject of Christopher saying she asked him to lie. She said: "He is all mixed up. I remember it clearly as I had gotten on a bus at 11.10 pm and he was not home when I got home." She said she went to look for him at 12.45am as she was worried. He came in full of it, whatever that means. I presume drugs or alcohol. We discussed the new locks mum had fitted in August 1984 and the mystery of the missing key. Kathleen had been there at the time it was being fitted.*

New locks being fitted on Mum's door had been a big deal at the time because John and Mum had been estranged from each other for a long time. But a couple of months before she died John had visited to make peace with her.

It went well, I believe, and a few weeks later they met again and Mum mentioned she could only use the Yale lock and not the Mortice lock which gave added security. John fitted a new lock for her. Mum was pleased at that.

Kathleen said: "Now that I come to think about it, when John was fitting it he made a point of showing me three mortice keys. When handing them to my ma, he said to me, you're my witness. I have given her three keys. So what happened to the other key?"

I said to Kathleen, "Well, she is dead now so I doubt we'll find out. Maybe she gave it to someone else other than a neighbour. I don't know, all I know is it would be good if we all got closure and justice for my mum."

Kathleen said a person well known to us both had been abusing mum. She had seen one of them with hands around Mum's neck. Another person, she said, used to steal from her. I have heard the key story so often; it's imprinted on my brain. But what does it mean? The killer took her keys? What?

18

A Cold Case Awakens

AT THE beginning of September 2017, over 12 months after Jane published my *Daily Record* story, I had a telephone call from a newspaper reporter who started asking me lots of questions. I was confused. How did he get my number? He said he found it on the internet and as I was self-employed at that time, it made sense but I felt uneasy. I made a mental note to get my number removed from the internet. He wanted to talk about my mum and was rattling off questions. I was blunt.

"Why now?" I asked.

Then he dropped a bombshell. The police had made a breakthrough in the case. Could he come and see me? Reluctantly, I agreed. They wanted photos done of me. My natural instinct was to say no but if it helped to highlight Mum's case again I would swallow my nerves and do it.

The reporter cancelled our meeting. He did send his photographer though. Unknown to me there had already been two stories in the papers in recent weeks.

I was able to get a hold of the newspaper and was stunned to see my picture in the paper with an interview with a reporter I'd never heard off.

I contacted the editor and within minutes the reporter called me and told me he'd used a pseudonym and could not contain the breakthrough information because it came from a source who was a police officer and he could lose his job if his superiors found out he'd been passing information to a journalist.

I felt duped. I don't feel his tactics to speak to me had been ethical. I spoke to Jane about it but she was non-committal. Every reporter is different, she said, and he was just doing his job.

I asked if she knew about the breakthrough and she said she did but police were asking journalists to hold off until the family had been contacted.

She hinted that there had been movement on the case and the police were hopeful of a result.

Jane admitted this information was not public knowledge and only journalists with good contacts were aware.

I asked what she meant by contacts but Jane is a

professional journalist and she didn't want to discuss that. I had to respect her decision.

Not long after this a team from the Forensic Services Cold Case Review Team (CCRT) came to visit me.

The CCRT had been set up in 2013 by the Scottish Police Authority – who are the governance body overseeing the work of the newly created single police force in Scotland. Instead of eight separate forces in their geographical areas, they would become one – Police Scotland.

The CCRT was just one of many new departments created and their job was to review cold cases from as far back as the 1960s and up to 2019.

Working in partnership with Police Scotland's Homicide Governance Review Team and the Crown and Procurator Fiscal Service National Homicide team they discussed and prioritised 48 cases. The team would eventually go on to work on over 70 cases including the Lockerbie bombing enquiry.

Mum's case was one of the homicide cases they had decided to look at and review again.

There were three members of the cold case team present, Kenny McCubbbin, Jim Findland and Angela Gentles. They explained in great detail why they were there and what the next steps would be. Understandably they were cautiously optimistic and said advances in technology meant there was a lot they could do.

They told me they were revisiting the murder and had already started the long, arduous task of speaking to all the witnesses from 1984 who were still alive. Forensics, they said, was just one strand of the investigation and there would also be 'old-fashioned' detective work going on too. They had a mammoth task on their hands and were aware the family had been torn apart and were very sympathetic to the situation.

To this day, I appreciate their empathy and handling of the situation. They understood that despite the passage of time our grief as a family was still strong and that having a resolution to mum's murder was something we all needed.

At the first visit they wanted to go over my statements from 1984 and confirm the details were correct, which they were.

I was also asked to provide a DNA sample for testing which I was happy to do. They said everyone in the family who was still alive would also be asked. It's standard procedure, they said. We chatted about my thoughts on the events of 1984 and my thoughts as they stood in 2017 and I repeated that I still believed someone in my family knew more than they were letting on.

I could not accept, I told them, that my mum would willingly go home with a strange man who had accosted her in the street. It is and will always remain my firm belief that either Kathleen or Christopher knew and introduced my mum to her killer.

They appointed a Family Liaison Officer (FLO) to deal with us and keep the family updated on what was happening. This was quite positive compared to 1984 when we had no-one. I know there is a lot of criticism directed at Police Scotland but my experience with them has always been fairly pleasant. I wish I could say the same about Strathclyde Police as the force was known then.

On the way out they mentioned they were going to visit Kathleen. I later learned they could not get an answer at her door and this would become a regular pattern unfortunately. She did everything she could to avoid the police.

On one visit to her she told me they had eventually managed to get her and she got so angry at their line of questioning and asked them to leave. I felt embarrassed. The team were trying everything they could to solve the murder and Kathleen was acting as if she was the main suspect.

I tried to make her understand that they were trying to help. She was angry and evasive and wanted to know why it was all being dragged up again.

At this point, I had no idea forensic science would be key to unlocking the mystery. As far as I was concerned, it was still a boots on the ground approach to policing and while I wasn't feeling particularly hopeful that they would get a result I was enormously grateful they were trying.

On another visit, we got around to talking about Christopher's allegations and how he said he didn't think the police believed him.

Jim Findland said, "Do you not think police would have taken a note of that, Gina?"

"Well you would think so but there is no record of me going into the station to report what he said," I replied.

The silence was uncomfortable after that.

I mentioned my diaries and allowed the team to read them.

They said they would be checking out everything they read and heard and that the investigation would be ongoing for some time.

As they were leaving they asked if I'd spoken to a reporter and I said yes, I had. I was hoping they would tell me how this journalist had the information before we, the family, did but they didn't ask what the conversation was about. I guess they didn't have to since it had appeared in the *Daily Mail*.

Years later they told me they knew the information had been leaked by a police officer to the journalist. And it was clear it was Christopher who was interviewed for their article.

By 2017, it had been more than three decades since

Mum was murdered, and in all that time, we had been left with nothing but unanswered questions. Then, just when I had begun to believe I might never know the truth, a breakthrough came. And it was a newspaper who broke the news to us.

The newspaper article said a man had come forward to the police, admitting something we had long suspected but never been able to prove. According to the paper, the man confessed that back in 1984, during the original investigation, he had provided a false alibi for someone close to Mum. After all those years, the solid story he had told in 1984 began to crumble.

Mum had been found strangled in her flat, the door locked behind her, no sign of a struggle. It had always pointed to someone she knew. We believed it from the very start, and so did the police, even if they could never prove it. They had a few suspects, but the problem was always the same. No one could be tied to the crime scene, and certain people, suspicious as they were, had strong alibis, backed up by more than one witness.

Now, with this new confession, the police finally had cause to reopen the case. A senior officer described it as a major development, saying it blew a hole in the original alibi, removing one of the key puzzles that had shielded a suspect all these years. It was, he said, the first real breakthrough in decades.

Of course, nothing is ever simple. The new information had to be tested, checked against what was left of the original evidence, and cross-referenced with other witnesses. The police also planned to review whether any of the exhibits from the original investigation could still yield forensic evidence. Even so, for the first time in a long time, it felt like someone was actually listening, like the case was no longer forgotten at the bottom of a dusty pile on a shelf.

When the news broke, I spoke to the reporter writing the story and tried to explain what it felt like. Losing Mum had been devastating. Losing her to murder was worse. But being denied justice for more than 30 years, left with no closure, no truth, that had been its own kind of life sentence. Writing my book, Diamonds and Pearls, had been a way to try and make sense of it all, a way to put some order into the chaos we were left with.

For years, I had been afraid I would die without ever knowing who had really taken Mum from us. Now, for the first time in what felt like a lifetime, there was a weakness in the chain of lies told by some.

Maybe, just maybe, justice was finally within reach.

It was also apparent to us but not the public that it was Christopher who had gone to the police with new information. And he had told them his mum asked him to lie about her whereabouts on the night Mum was last seen alive.

After the article appeared I dropped in to see Kathleen

and take her some shopping. We talked about the story and about the time of Mum's death. I asked her if she thought someone we knew had done it. No, was her response.

"I know everyone my ma knew," she said. "I think it [the killer] must be from Partick. Mum's clothing had to be identified on the night she was found. There was a clump of her hair."

I remembered Kathleen telling me she thought perhaps someone had punched Mum during a fight and as she bled easily they left not realising she was dead.

I asked the CCR team about this and was told there is no connection to that claim in this investigation.

Christopher came to visit me during this time and was in a talkative mood. He wanted to talk about his mum and granny. All I could do was listen but I felt sad. He was gripped with guilt and paranoia and said someone his granny knew had killed her.

A few days later Kathleen called me and said the police had just left. They had been asking a lot of questions, nothing to worry about, she said.

"I remember the night clearly," Kathleen told me. "The last time Ma was seen alive, as I wasn't drinking. The CID wanted to know how she usually dressed. I told them unless she was going to a dance she would dress casual. I told them about someone stealing from her and told them I thought I knew who killed her."

My mind was racing. Kathleen was voicing her suspicions for the first time but I didn't tell her I thought she was part of it.

Something stopped me. I got the feeling she was trying to detract attention from herself by suddenly talking about what she thinks happened.

When she called me back in another couple of days to say the police had been round twice in two days, I wasted no time.

"You told the police on Wednesday who you thought it was but for years you have kept quiet." I was aware my tone was accusing.

"I know," she replied.

When I asked her to tell me who she suspected, she answered, "I will explain on Saturday when I see you."

As planned, I visited her on Saturday afternoon and we talked again about the police. She was annoyed with how long they were taking and asked them to leave. She confided in me then and told me who she believed killed our mum, a name she had kept to herself all these years for reasons I'll never understand.

She said the police told her to put the thought out of her head. In other words, this person wasn't a suspect and could not be tied to the case. She said she needed to take a sleeping tablet after the police left.

"Understandable," I replied. "It opens old memories."

She refused to say anymore. I often wonder what her

endgame was – was it to throw me and the police off the scent? By pushing suspicion onto someone else?

On Christmas Day 2017, I went to visit Christopher with a Christmas card and some sweets. He said the police wanted to know about the missing two hours on the night mum was murdered.

He was going back to live with his mum and suddenly his allegations seemed to disappear.

I later found out from the police they had attempted to question him about half a dozen times but could never find him at home.

A year passed since the investigation had been reopened and I saw both Kathleen and Christopher very infrequently. They only seemed to want to see me if they'd been fighting. To be honest, I felt relieved I wasn't being dragged into their drama constantly. It helped me to put some distance between them, me and my mum's murder. For a long time that year, I felt like a normal everyday person who wasn't carrying the weight of the world on her shoulders.

With every day that passed without any news from the police I felt that anything Kathleen knew or did would never be discovered.

In January 2019 came sad news.

Christopher had died. He was only 52.

He had been back staying with his mum and everything seemed rosy between them. I felt so sorry for him. If only he'd sought help he might have lived a lot longer. 52 is really no age at all. I did go and ask the police if I should destroy my diary now he was dead and was told to keep them.

Kenny McCubbin was the investigating officer and had been looking at Mum's case for years. I know he was very passionate about it and wanted to solve the case. He took the time to explain the difficulties the police in 1984 would've had with it; there was no forensic capabilities other than fingerprints, no mobile phones, no CCTV and forensic evidence was not something they thought about.

But Kenny was determined. He said Mum was a defenceless woman who should have been safe in her own home. I know every detective wants to solve the crimes they're assigned and in Kenny I saw a tenacious and dedicated officer.

My doubts began to disappear. For the first time I felt a tiny spark of hope.

I had no way of knowing that the police were keeping their cards close to their chest and in the background they were making huge strides in solving this case.

19

Breakthrough

IT WAS December 2019 and I was staying in a lovely hotel overlooking the water in Arrochar, a little village in the Argyll and Bute area of Scotland. The water was rippling gently as I stood looking out the window. The moon was casting a light on the water and it was a very mild evening for December which is usually bleak and chilly in Scotland.

My daughter and I had come for a visit for her birthday. My baby girl was going to be 50! Life was passing by so quickly. It comes and goes in the blink of an eye. I had lived longer on this earth than my mother and my daughter wasn't far behind.

I am blessed that my daughter is my best friend. We do lots together; we laugh, we cry, we have fun, we have arguments but above anything else we love and care for each other and we have a good relationship. I am not my mother's daughter in that respect. I was determined the sins of the mother and father would not be passed down. I like to think I have succeeded in that at least.

We were having a perfect evening. We had enjoyed a lovely dinner and admired the beautiful Christmas tree with its lavish decorations sparkling away in the corner of the dining room. Afterwards we listened to some music, watched some television and chatted until the wee small hours of the morning. We spoke for so long our words were slurring with tiredness.

As I watched the river flow, I thought this had been the most perfect evening I'd had in a long time. I felt content and at peace.

The next morning my mobile phone kept ringing. I didn't recognise the number so decided to ignore it. Besides, I was getting ready for breakfast and I was hungry. Whoever was calling was persistent. I said to my daughter I should answer as it must be important.

It was a police officer. He asked if he could see me that day. I didn't think there was anything untoward, there was nothing in his manner to suggest anything significant. I guess I assumed it was another pointless update, a merry-go-round I had been on for 30 years. We arranged to meet at my home at 2pm.

On the drive home I became quite sombre. It suddenly struck me that perhaps something had happened after all because I had only seen them two weeks before and there had been no major update then. Before I knew it, I was home and pacing the floor. I was a bag of nerves wondering what had happened.

Two officers in plain clothes appeared at my door. Detective Superintendent Suzanne Chow, now a Chief Superintendent, is a very experienced cold case police officer. She was the officer in charge of Mum's case. The SIO in police speak. I knew it was something very serious when I saw her enter with Angela Gentles. Usually it was Kenny who dealt with the family.

They told me to sit down. I'm glad I did.

"We wanted to let you know we will be charging someone in connection with your mother's death," DS Chow said.

I let out a gasp. Shock engulfed my body. Words I never expected to hear in my lifetime. We. Have. Someone. For. Your. Mother's. Murder.

I began to shake and started to cry. My mind was in turmoil. A million questions were rattling around in my head so fast I couldn't even muster up enough voice to ask one. Every emotion was coursing through me; I was shocked, happy, sad, curious but stunned. Sensing my inability to ask them anything, the two women gently explained that they were sure they had finally nailed the right person. They couldn't go into specifics at that point but wanted to let us know before the media were told in a few hours. Could I let the rest of the family know?

As Suzanne was leaving I made my feelings known that I was not accusing anyone in my family of killing my mum but I did believe that someone in my family knew who was in the company of my Mum the night she died.

The two police officers didn't say anything in reply to that. What could they say? As far as they were concerned they had their man.

After they left I called my daughters and son and then decided I'd go round to Kathleen's in person to tell her. The Cullens were told via my sister Marie and also Martin as he was the police contact too.

Kathleen cried a little but she was never one for showing emotion.

At 4pm the police called and said they'd arrested a man and he was in custody. They couldn't give us any more information. It felt like 1984 all over again.

Mum's face was on all the news programmes but they kept it very brief just saying a man had been arrested in connection with a murder 35 years before. The newspaper headlines were bigger, but they printed a lot of old information – I suspect to pad out the story since legally they couldn't say very much.

I would soon be getting a very swift lesson on media law in Scotland whether I wanted to or not. I spoke to Jane Hamilton and told her I was shocked. This much was true. It was all very overwhelming. For many years

I had convinced myself I would go to my own grave never knowing who killed my mum but this new development gave me hope.

Soon I had a name. Graham McGill. It seemed that justice was finally coming for my mum.

20

Eureka

AFTER GRAHAM McGill made his first appearance in court charged with the murder of my mum, the police told us the Crown Office and Procurator Fiscal Service (COPFS) would be taking over dealing with the family. I was to attend a meeting at their office in the Gorbals and it was at this meeting they told me a new FLO was being assigned and Kenny was retiring.

I was sad he wasn't going to see it through to the bitter end. He had worked so hard on the case.

I know that my mum's case meant a lot to him and he was keen to see someone brought to justice. I will always be enormously grateful to Kenny and all the officers who worked on Mum's case during that particular enquiry. Without their tenacity and determination, McGill might have been left free all of his life.

During this meeting with more new faces and some old, I again raised my suspicions regarding Kathleen. I refused to let it go, my gut was telling me to keep going. Every instinct in my body was screaming. While I was pleased they had someone I still felt as if my sister had to answer for her evasiveness and asking Christopher to lie about her whereabouts the night my mum was last seen alive.

I'm pretty sure the people in the room that day were baffled by this crazy old woman who didn't seem at all as satisfied as they thought I should be that the end was in sight. But I was determined not to let it go.

"I know much more than the police do, I've been around it for years, around Kathleen, I know what was being said. There was a time my home was a hub for the family over the years and I listened to everything. I feel you are missing something important," I told them.

The cold case team had actually told me they believed Christopher did know something but when I said more than one person was involved they told me I was wrong. To this day the feeling has never left me. I don't think it ever will.

Even though they had someone, I was in turmoil. Every day I waited for the knock on my door telling me they had found an accomplice for McGill. The PF told me things would go very quiet during this period as they worked to put the case together for court.

I knew nothing of the criminal justice world and assumed once the police handed over their files it would be straight to court but clearly I was wrong. On television everything seems so fast, so cut and dried. Incident happens, police investigate, murderer caught, in court and sent to prison. The End.

What I didn't realise was there would be more work going on in the background to strengthen the case against the accused and that every witness had to go through precognition. In Scots Law, this is done by the Procurator Fiscal staff to go over witness statements to determine whether there is enough evidence to proceed to trial. These interviews are done in private and the lawyers can ask questions the police did not.

I'm told they can also ask for your views on whether the case should go to trial or not but this seems very much like a courtesy especially when they have strong forensic evidence. DNA can place a person at the scene of a crime but it doesn't mean they did it. A fact I actually pointed out to the police when they told me they had McGill's DNA on items from Mum's flat.

I think at that point I was still very naive about how the science works. Even now my knowledge is quite basic.

I should have been happy they had an accused and I was, deep down. But I couldn't let go of my suspicions about someone else being involved. When I left the fiscal's office that day I decided I was going to put the whole rotten business out of my mind. No matter what I thought, what I felt like they'd missed, they were dismissing me and making me feel like I'd got it wrong.

It was destroying me. I felt like I was going mad. Why wouldn't anyone listen to me?

I have since rationalised it in my head that as far as the police and the crown office were concerned, they had 'their man' and a decades old mystery was no longer such.

I'm aware I sound ungrateful and I'm truly not. I cannot argue with the science and I'm satisfied they have the right person but there are still many many questions I need answered.

The period between McGill's first appearance in court and actually going to trial was torture. Under Scots Law, when a person is fully committed for trial, the prosecutors have 110 days to bring the case to court. This meant that McGill should have been going to trial later in 2020.

But in March 2020, the COVID pandemic broke out. The world just stopped. All jury trials were suspended almost immediately. Some trials did resume later in the year but there were many more put off due to the pandemic and the ensuing backlog. McGill's trial was to be heard in the High Court in Glasgow. It turned into a nightmare for us as a family.

I understand with the pandemic and social distancing going on that the wheels of justice were turning very slowly, but for those of us going through the faceless, soulless bureaucracy that is the justice system it felt cruel.

His plea hearing, which would've taken all of 15 minutes, was delayed at least half a dozen times. I was so distraught by it I actually wrote to the Scottish Government to ask if it was acceptable that families were being put through the wringer with postponed hearings while those accused and maybe those innocent were languishing in prison remand cells.

I even wrote to Nicola Sturgeon who was the First Minister at the time to ask if the Government had considered the impact it was having on families with court cases not going ahead, in particular for heinous crimes. I told her bereaved families were struggling to cope and highlighted all the times McGill's court dates were postponed. The waiting felt the same as it did waiting for my mum's body to be released by the police for burial.

She never did reply to me but I believe my letter was passed to the Procurator Fiscal as it was shortly afterwards that McGill made his plea appearance. I have no idea if the former First Minister intervened because you hear politicians say they don't get involved in legal matters so I doubt I will ever know.

McGill first appeared in court on December 5th, 2019. He should've appeared eight days later for a second appearance. It was February 2021 before he entered his plea to the court: Not Guilty. This meant he would be going to trial.

We were told by the prosecutor a space had suddenly opened up and the trial itself would begin in April. I felt nervous but anxious for it to happen quickly. We were warned to expect distressing details and offered help from Victim Support.

I had communicated over 100 times with the court. In total there were 13 cancellations before he finally stood in the dock.

While I felt the officials dealt with us with great empathy, after all they were under great pressure too from hundreds of families and lawyers, it didn't take away from the pain. I needed McGill to stand trial! I needed to know the truth once and for all.

21

The Anatomy of Proof and Justice

AFTER 35 years of wondering what had happened to my mother and why she was murdered, the end seemed to be in sight. I was told the police had put forward a good case against McGill and that there was irrefutable proof he was guilty. I decided to leave my own judgement until I'd heard all of the evidence.

Police had carried out reviews in 1999, 2002 to 2004 and 2008. Each time the productions stored carefully from the crime were examined by scientists using the latest methods available to them but the secrets buried inside the items stubbornly refused to reveal themselves.

In 2014 they decided to launch another review. Science had moved on in leaps and bounds in the seven years since my mum's case was last looked at. As a family we weren't aware police had decided to look at everything again.

DNA24 is described as the 'gold standard of profiling' according to the forensic scientist working on Mum's case, Joanne Cochrane. And it's thanks to the investment and opening of Scotland's £6m profiling facility in 2015 that mum's murderer could be identified. The facility is said to be the most advanced in Europe and the best.

Prior to DNA24, scientists could only look at 11 areas of a person's DNA and the European standard is 17. This allows scientists to extract DNA from smaller or lower quality samples which increases the odds of obtaining results.

While the facilities might be the best in Europe at least, Joanne issued a warning to the police and Crown Office. The problem with decades old evidence is it is highly fragile and difficult to examine; meaning even the gentlest of touches could destroy it.

While she was happy to proceed, Joanne warned it could be the end of the road if the items became damaged during examination.

It was a cigarette butt recovered from mum's flat that provided police with their 'eureka' moment. When you smoke you are possibly transferring saliva onto the end of the cigarette. This particular cigarette was an Embassy – and the police knew Mum smoked

Woodbine – so the team felt it was an important piece of preserved evidence that may possibly lead to the identity of her killer.

Despite being previously tested, the cigarette this time provided a full DNA profile. Graham McGill was on the DNA database having been previously convicted of serious sexual offences including rape and attempted rape. Is he the killer? Did he murder my mum in her own home on 26 September 1984?

This man was a serial offender who preyed on lone women as they went about their business. I think about Mum walking home, shoes in hand, chips tucked under her arm, maybe a little merry from the drink but happy with her lot in life encountering this monster. The devil.

The police were so sure he was the culprit but they had to prove it. His DNA alone was not proof he carried out the actual killing and then came a problem they were not anticipating: McGill had a solid alibi.

On the night Mum was murdered he was officially classed as being inside prison serving a six-year sentence for a sexual offence. The detectives were deflated and baffled. It didn't make sense to them at all. McGill wasn't released from the Edinburgh prison until 5th October 1984, three days after my brother, Martin, found mum's body in her flat.

When they asked the Crown office if the DNA on the cigarette was enough to proceed to court they said no and refused to prosecute him. They needed more evidence.

Joanne went back to the evidence room and again dug out what she has described as a "time capsule of DNA" and looked at scrapings from mum's nails, her hair, her dress, her bra and the ligature used to strangle her.

She believed whoever had tied the knot may have touched the material inside and left behind their DNA. Piece by piece she unravelled the knot, photographing it at every stage, and eventually exposed the fabric inside. Here they found more DNA belonging to McGill. The odds of it belonging to anyone else was one billion to one. Traces of his semen were found on my Mum's dress. This I find particularly distressing for obvious reasons.

DNA was also found on the discarded bra detectives in 1984 had found in a communal garden. Again, it belonged to McGill.

But despite all of the scientific evidence that placed him at the scene it was still not enough; how could he have murdered mum if he was 60 miles away in prison?

Kenny McCubbin was tasked with solving the mystery if police had any hope of being able to take McGill to trial. In 1984, computers were scarce. Paperwork was handwritten and filed away in cabinets. When Mum died, HMP Edinburgh was being rebuilt and much of that paperwork was lost. Kenny ended up in the

National Records Office of Scotland where he discovered the Governor's journals.

Next to Graham McGill's name and prison number was the acronym 'TFF' which meant 'Training for Freedom'. Typically prisoners who were on the TFF program would be allowed weekend leave – two days. McGill, it transpired, also had three days pre-parole leave added on, meaning he didn't return to prison until September 27th, 1984.

But the police didn't stop there. They wanted to make sure their case was as strong as possible when McGill appeared in front of a jury. They interviewed his ex-wife, Suzanne Russell, who is now deceased, and she told them McGill had confessed to her in 1988 that he had murdered a woman "because he wanted to know what it felt like to kill someone" and told her he was actually shocked at how long it took my mum to die.

Suzanne said McGill told her he had strangled Mum with her tights after going back to her flat and wasn't worried about the police being after him because she was on her own, she didn't have anybody and she was a prostitute.

She didn't believe him, she said, because he was just saying it to threaten her because she wanted to leave him. Suzanne said she met him in 1985 and married him in 1993 before leaving in 1999.

I feel no malice or ill thoughts towards Suzanne. She

was terrified of McGill who had threatened to kill her if she ever told anyone or if she left him. She had no idea who his victim was and I would imagine even if she'd gone to police before they found her, she wouldn't have been able to give them any more detail. It would've been like looking for a needle in a haystack considering the number of unsolved female murders in Scotland.

I had waited for this trial for a long time. I was stuck somewhere between anticipation and fear. I wasn't sure about going to court. It was an alien world to me. I knew for sure I did not want to see any crime scene pictures that I knew they would be showing to the jury. Did that mean the public would see too? I had no idea how it all worked.

I woke up that first day undecided if I was going or not. I kept telling myself I was stronger than this and for over 35 years I had been searching and looking for answers, scrutinising everything I'd heard, sleuthing like the amateur I am, determined to keep her memory alive and hoping and praying her murderer would be found and punished.

Now it was about to happen and I was annoyed with myself. I was actually having to convince myself to face going. Could I face what was about to unfold? Did I really want to hear it all? A picture of Mum flashed in my mind, I felt she was nagging me, urging me to go and see it through. I ordered a taxi and headed off to Glasgow High Court.

Kathleen, who at this point was walking with the aid of a zimmer frame, had been cited as a witness so I wasn't allowed to sit with her and Elaine. I was ushered into a room by one of the PF assistants and told to wait until I was called by the courtroom attendants.

My head was reeling. I took a look at my surroundings. It was a dark room full of highly polished wood panels. The ceiling was decorated with ornate cornices and in the centre was this huge light. The furniture was dark oak, I think. There was a bookcase, a heavy table, leather chairs held together with brass tacks. It was meant to look grand I expect but to me it was dark and gloomy. The only nod to modern times was the water machine in the corner with the flimsy plastic cups. I wondered if the public rooms were as extravagant or much more basic.

My heart felt heavy with the weight of what was to come then I looked out the window and could see the archway of Glasgow Green opposite. This was the area my dad lived. Albion Street was not far away at all. It's now classed as part of the very upmarket area of the Merchant City – an area much like the room I'm sitting in now. 18th-century buildings renovated to occupy classy and trendy designer boutiques, bistros, cocktail bars and restaurants.

Across the bridges is the Central Mosque in the Gorbals and further along is one of my dad's homes before he married my mum in Hollybrook Street. My thoughts turned to them and how sad it was for them in their lives and how their separation affected so many people and the ultimate consequences for my mum. I've spent my life believing if she'd stayed with my dad she probably would not have encountered McGill.

My train of thought was interrupted by the Procurator Fiscal and one of his assistants coming to talk to me. Aside from explaining the procedure they told me I was free to leave the courtroom anytime I wanted to or needed to.

Once inside the court you sat anywhere you wanted to and I was surprised to find it so empty looking save for a few officials and possibly some journalists. I had expected it to be full of people.

I hadn't realised that where I was sitting was right behind the dock where the accused sits. I was aware I would be seeing the man accused of murdering my mum for the first time in the flesh and my stomach rolled.

I didn't recognise people sitting in the court and wondered if they were relatives of his.

I first saw his bald head appear as he emerged from the cells below the dock. He was head down and chained to a prison officer.

In all honesty, I felt absolutely nothing when I saw him for the first time. Perhaps I'm naive but at the point I was still thinking innocent until proven guilty. I just looked at him and thought here you are just a wee fat balding aging man finally having to answer for the crime you are being accused of.

I tried to picture him as a 22-year-old killer but it was difficult. He was shorter than I anticipated too. How does a young person turn into a killer? Did he know about the damage he'd caused? The pain he'd inflicted? Did he think about my mum ever? Did he feel even the slightest bit of remorse?

Martin Cullen was the first to be called to give evidence and I remember him talking about the hell of finding our mum dead in her flat. I do remember Martin said that in his police statement in 1984, he had told police Mum was "scared" about a month before her death. I made a mental note to find out more about that.

Martin Cullen and his late partner, June Brittle, discovered Mum dead on October 2nd, 1984. The jury were told Mum had been murdered by a strip of cloth that had been wound around her neck several times. Martin said he could not get an answer and noticed a strange smell when he turned up at the flat.

Prosecutor Alex Prentice QC asked Mr Cullen what it was like and he replied, "The most horrible smell you could imagine." Martin said he was forced to kick the door in, even after he'd got the spare key from a neighbour. June went into the flat with him and left screaming.

The joint minutes of agreed facts were read out to the jury by Alex Prentice QC who was prosecuting the case. "When she was found the victim was lying on a bed on her back with her right arm lying on the side of the bed and her legs apart," he stated. "The body was in a state of putrefaction, especially of the face. A ligature was tied tightly round her neck and knotted on the side and deeply indented into the flesh of her neck.

"There was no trace of blood about the body or bed. A tie from a lady's dress or an apron passed round the neck three times with two knots in it."

Mum, the pathologists said, had died five days before her body was discovered.

Kathleen was next to take the stand and I, again, felt the anger bubbling in me because I knew she would not be treated as a suspect during this trial. I wonder if the prosecutor even knew about the missing two hours Kathleen refused to speak about. I doubt it. She told the court she had been at the pub with Mum that night and said Mum wasn't drunk but she was happy.

Kathleen admitted under cross-examination from McGill's defence counsel, Sarah Livingstone, that sometimes Mum took people home with her, especially after the pub.

I only found out during the trial that in her original police statement Kathleen had told them that Mum had, on one occasion, invited two men back to her flat. One she knew and one she didn't.

My understanding is Ms Livingstone was trying to convince the jury that Mum would indeed let anyone into her home.

I tried not to let that bother me as I knew it was her job to discredit whatever the prosecution came up with. Thankfully we had been warned pre-trial that we might hear a lot of things that were upsetting.

I remember feeling quite calm about that. I may not have experience of courts but I had watched enough crime dramas on television to understand that even the purest of victims can be eviscerated when it comes to the accused defending themselves.

After Kathleen gave evidence it was the lunch recess. I thought to myself it had all been routine for the first day and wasn't as bad as I thought but of course the real drama was waiting for me outside.

I thought that, as a lot of years had gone by and a lot of water under the bridge, my divided family would come together at the court. After all, we were all there for the same reason – our mother.

Whenever we had trouble I always tried to remind myself that my loss was their loss too and in the most horrible of circumstances, especially for Martin. I thought our past differences could be put to rest or at the very least put to one side while we were at court. How wrong I was! If anything it was worse than I imagined it would be.

I had decided I would just sit in a room away from my siblings as there were some there I had not spoken to for a number of years. A court official found me a room and left me there with a bottle of water.

After about 10 minutes, Kathleen spotted me through the window. In as loud a voice as she could muster, in her strong Glasgow accent, she shouted, "Gina, come ootside! Me and Elaine are goin fur a fag."

I gestured to her 'five minutes' with my hand but didn't want to seem rude so ventured outside. My niece seemed uncomfortable as they stood puffing away. I was not aware that Martin, Carol and Patricia were standing close by.

Elaine said the atmosphere was tense. I didn't want to get involved and went back inside. I took my seat as other people started to come into the courtroom.

The last witness was a taxi driver David Seager who knew mum as 'Wee Mary'. He remembered seeing Mum walk in front of his taxi carrying her shoes in her hand. When asked if he saw a man standing outside a shoe shop following Mum he replied, yes.

According to David, every time Mum walked away, the man was behind her.

The proceedings ended abruptly because McGill, who has a heart condition, felt unwell and the Judge, Lord Burns, said he needed to be examined by a doctor.

After about 15 minutes he said court was dismissed for the day and we were all to go home.

I telephoned the PF's office when I got home to tell them I wouldn't be attending any more of the trial.

A member from the family liaison team called me back and suggested that if I did not want to attend she could call me every day with an update on the day's proceedings.

The next day was crucial, she said, as my sisters Carol and Patricia would be giving evidence as well as Suzanne Russell, McGill's ex-wife, and Joanne Cochrane.

True to her word, she called me and told me about the forensic case and Suzanne's testimony. She asked if I would be attending the next day but I said I wasn't sure and she suggested that perhaps I should as it would be the closing statements from the prosecution and defence and the jury would be going out to begin their deliberations before delivering a verdict on the Friday.

I didn't fully understand the significance of Suzanne Russell until I read the newspaper which had detailed the proceedings the day before.

The following is an extract from the *Daily Record* from 7 April 2021:

Suzanne Russell, 55, from Glasgow, told prosecutor Alex Prentice QC: "He said he was round the pub for a drink and he said a woman wouldn't leave him alone and kept pestering him.

"He decided to go back to her flat with her. He said he had murdered her.

"He said he strangled her and said he just wanted to know what it felt like to kill someone.

"He said he used her tights and said he was shocked how long it took to actually murder her."

The High Court in Glasgow heard that McGill and Ms Russell were in a relationship from 1985 and married in 1993.

Mr Prentice asked her: "Did you say something to him?"

She replied: "Yes, were you not worried the police would be after you? He said, 'No, not at all'."

The prosecutor then said: "Did he give a reason why?" and the witness replied: "He said he wasn't worried about it as she had no one and was more like a prostitute.

Ms Russell was asked her reaction to this and said: "I didn't believe him. He threatened me and said if I ever told anyone he would kill me and if I ever reported it or tried to leave him that's what would happen."

Under cross-examination by defence counsel, Sarah Livingstone asked Ms Russell if she wanted McGill to get into trouble and she replied: "No."

Miss Livingstone asked: "The confession didn't happen, did it?"

She replied: "I didn't know if it happened but he said it did."

Miss Livingston said: "You didn't believe he murdered anyone?"

She replied: "I didn't believe him, I was only told and I wasn't allowed to report."

The trial before judge Lord Burns continues.

I read on:

Forensic Scientist Joanne Cochrane told the court a number of forensic investigations were undertaken to try to find DNA other than Mum's from items at the scene.

Four previous attempts to recover samples had been made between 1984 and 2008. The most recent was in 2014 and continued until 2020.

Ms Cochrane said that the ligature had been examined before but there was one knot in the cord which had never been opened.

She told the court: "We felt that within the knot might be protected from contamination. We felt there was a possibility of receiving DNA from within the knot.

"We did it very slowly and took photographs at all stages. It was very difficult to unfasten."

The jury heard that previous examinations of the cord had only found Mary's DNA and a trace sample that it was then not possible to analyse.

Analysis carried out by her and a colleague found a mixed DNA profile with a major profile attributed to Mary and a minor one to Mr McGill.

She said that the likelihood of the DNA belonging to someone other than the accused was 85,000 to one.

The chance of DNA on the cigarette butt and the dress not being from Mr McGill was one billion to one.

And for a black bra, which was found abandoned outside, it was 320 to one.

Retired police officer Brian Foster told the court he was part of the CID team that investigated the crime in 1984.

He said: "Whoever had committed the murder had locked Mary's door leaving her dead inside. We never found Mary's keys."

The jurors were shown a seven-minute video of the interior of Mary's flat.

It showed her lying on her back on her bed with a ligature wrapped around her neck. Her dentures were lying on the floor beside the bed.

****

The next day I went in and listened to both sides present their closing arguments. I was not prepared for a big picture to flash up on the screen of the ligature used to strangle Mum. I felt nauseous looking at it. I looked around to see if any of my siblings were there but I couldn't see them.

In his closing speech to the jury, Alex Prentice said the crime was sexually motivated.

Mr Prentice said, "Mary McLaughlin was someone who was friendly and trusting and I would suggest that ultimately brought about her death.

"She trusted whoever was in her flat on September 26, 1984, The brutal attack on her indicates force."

McGill did not give evidence, but his defence team read out a statement from a former neighbour of Ms McLaughlin.

Isobel Barnes, who has since died, told police in October 1984 that she saw a man in Mary's flat four or five days before she died.

The witness told officers that the man, who she described as in his 20s or 30s, was sitting on a couch. A woman, who she thought was Mary but whose face she could not make out, was standing behind him.

Referring to the statement, Mr Prentice said, "There is no evidence as to who this person was. Mary McLaughlin being a trusting and friendly person, she often invited people back.

"She was someone who would go out and meet people and seek a little happiness in her life and that inevitably led to people going back to her flat," Mr Prentice continued.

"Semen found on her dress suggests a sexual encounter of some sort and Mary McLaughlin was killed in the late part of 26 September, 1984 into 27 September, 1984. You can conclude that she was murdered by a ligature tied round her neck. The only just verdict in this case is a verdict of guilty."

In her closing speech, defence counsel Sarah Livingstone told jurors there was no doubt Ms McLaughlin was murdered, but said they were being asked to speculate about who was responsible.

Ms Livingstone said the Crown produced "absolutely no eyewitnesses" and presented a case based on circumstantial evidence. She urged the jury not to rely on the forensic evidence.

Ms Livingstone said, "DNA is not a magic solution to solve a crime, no matter how much the prosecution want it to be.

"You don't have to touch anything for your DNA to be on it. It can be put on to items by secondary transfer."

She said that Mum led a chaotic lifestyle which meant "she may have exposed herself to dangers".

She also asked the jurors to consider why a taxi driver who saw a man following Mum did not mention a scar when describing him. Graham McGill has a distinctive scar from one ear down to his chin."

She added the reason for the omission was that it wasn't her client who was "stalking" Mum on the night she died.

"You cannot be satisfied that the person who is responsible for the brutal, horrendous murder of Mary McLaughlin was Graham McGill," she concluded.

I'd never heard of this mystery man seen in Mum's flat before then. I asked Kathleen if she knew anything about that but as usual she evaded my questions.

"Jesus, Gina, ah cannae mind. I wasn't with Ma aw the time for fuck's sake. Maybe it was somebody fi the pub."

The next day I didn't go in for the verdict, I decided I'd wait until someone called me. The Crown Office liaison called me as soon as the verdict was delivered.

All I heard down the phone was 'guilty'. I was shaking and crying, my emotions were all over the place.

I could barely see through my tears as I called my children and grandchildren, who had never met Mary, to tell them the news. Although they were all happy for me there was sadness too for Mum. It had taken so long to get to this point, so much had happened, so many lives had been destroyed, so much grief – all because one man wanted to know what it felt like to kill a fellow human being.

I remember thinking to myself, 'You didn't even have the courage to choose a victim who would have challenged you, instead you picked on a defenceless older woman who would've been no match for you.'

The story should end there. As far as everyone is concerned, justice for Mary McLaughlin has been done. Her murderer is rotting in prison.

For me, it was not the end.

I did not have closure.

22

Is Anybody Listening?

IT IS all over. The case is 'done and dusted' for the Crown. Case closed. A triumph for them, the police and the justice system. It's truly amazing how science and technology has advanced so much since 1984 and will continue to move forward in ways we can only imagine.

It sends a strong message to those who have or are thinking about committing serious crimes. You will get caught. You will not escape justice. Even if your crime was 40 years ago and you think you're home and dry, justice will prevail. Mum's case was a stunning 'result' for law enforcement.

But it did not feel like a victory to me. Mum is still dead. She suffered horrifically in her final moments. I can't dwell on how she must have felt knowing she was going to die. It's too much.

On the day he was found guilty, I was left more confused than ever. I did not get the answers I was looking for, apart from the obvious forensic details. I can't help but feel suspicious there is a wider picture relating to her murder. I am convinced this heinous murder could have been solved many years ago if the dots had been joined together and people spoke the truth.

I accept the guilty verdict – the science doesn't lie. McGill's DNA is at the scene, on the murder weapon so to speak. I have no doubt he murdered Mum.

The court rightly focused on the forensic evidence – after all, the prosecution's goal is to secure a conviction.

My mind is in turmoil, I had so much more information gathered over the years than was led in evidence. A 35-year-old murder was tried in eight hours. My head can't wrap around that.

I wanted to know why he chose my mum. I wanted to know why he travelled from Edinburgh prison to Glasgow. Did he know someone in the area? Did he know someone who knew Mary? Was that how they were introduced? Or did he pick her at random? An old lady going home a little bit worse for the wear on a dark night and saw an easy target? Did she beg for her life? Try to reason with him? Did he regret her death? Does he know the impact her murder has had on her family?

Those are answers I'm never going to get.

I tried to move on after the trial. I tried to put everything into perspective and accept that mum's murder had finally been solved. I was happy for everyone, my family, the police, the prosecutors and the forensic scientists. So many people had contributed to ensuring McGill faced his day of reckoning.

I did an interview with Jane in the *Daily Record* after the trial and I think I spoke to the BBC too. It's all a blur, everything moved so fast but, as with all news, the next day it's chip paper. The world forgets and moves on. It's those of us living with it who continue to endure the pain and the reality of coming to terms with what had transpired since that day in 1984.

I visited Mum's grave after the trial. It's somewhere I've gone every couple of months since they died. I wanted to tell her we had found him, that the devil she encountered that night was finally facing his judgement.

For 40 years I felt my mum's presence with me many times. I always had a spiritual feeling that she was the driving force for me to continue, not to give up, even in my darkest times. Every street I walked she was walking with me. She was never far away from my thoughts.

In my life, I have found myself in many situations that were reminders of her. It felt like she was guiding me step by step – something I never had from her when she was alive. She never had that herself as a child nor when she became a mother herself.

As I stood at her grave I knew it was time to let her go, let her rest in peace. Finally.

But not just yet, a little voice niggled away at me. I felt I still had more to do for her.

The wait for the sentencing hearing a month later seemed to drag. I kept myself busy with my grandchildren and children. My husband and I would do things together: go for dinner, walks, coffees and we tried not to let Mum be the constant topic of conversation.

It sounds awful, but she had dominated virtually every day of my life for years and I knew I was driving myself crazier as the case went on.

Everyone talks about closure when a court case is finished but try as I might I didn't feel any sense of closure at all. I still felt as if the whole truth about her death and the lead up to it hadn't been revealed. I felt I could not move on until her full story was told and I had the answers I still needed. I know I wasn't the only one in my family who had questions.

I went to visit my little sister Marie after the trial and discovered that she felt the same way as I did and she wasn't scared to confront Kathleen.

The trial was clearly still fresh in both our minds and she said to me, "Did you see that McGill in the newspapers and on the telly?" She then let out a laugh. "And Kathleen all dressed up in her fur coat? What is she like, eh? I think she thought she was in a movie or something."

I just smiled and replied, "That's Kathleen for you."

Then Marie dropped a bombshell.

"That Graham McGill? I'm sure Christopher used to hang around with him in his younger days when Kathleen lived in the Wynford in Maryhill."

My jaw dropped but I didn't get a chance to speak as Marie continued without pausing for breath.

"I am almost positive I saw him in Kathleen's house with Christopher and a group of boys he hung around with. Christopher would've been about 17. This McGill was a bit older than him but I knew he had a girlfriend called Suzanne and he was going to get married to her. When I saw his picture in the paper, I said to myself, I know him. McGill is the double of his dad who I knew from Kathleen's bit. I'm sure it's the same Graham that Christopher knew."

I was shocked Marie had said all this. My little sister isn't one for gossiping but I wanted to try and be the sensible one so I replied, "We don't know for sure it is, Marie"

"I'm sure it is," she said.

I went to see her about 10 days later and she told me she'd bumped into an old friend on the bus. Of course anyone we met during that time wanted to speak about Mum's murder and the trial so Marie's friend brought it up.

She said she was glad to see someone had been done

for it and Marie said to her she was sure he was a friend of Christopher's. Her friend replied, "Was it not one of your other sisters who knew him? I'm sure it was."

At the end of February 2022, Kathleen had been discharged from hospital and was back home. I was giving Marie an update on her health and how she was keeping.

"She refused all help from social services because she said she didn't want them poking around her life."

Marie just laughed and said to tell her she was asking for her.

At my next visit to Kathleen I told her Marie was also feeling poorly but sent her regards. Kathleen said she wouldn't mind seeing her little sister as it had been a number of years since they last saw each other. It was soon arranged that I would take Marie to see Kathleen.

On that day, Elaine, Kathleen's daughter, was also there. There were hugs all round and then we all settled down for a natter.

At first it was just general chit chat about how they were both doing until Marie unexpectedly said, "Kathleen, that McGill? Was he not pally with Christopher? I am sure your Christopher knew him."

The room went silent. Kathleen jumped off her seat and said she needed to go to the toilet. When she returned a few moments later she said she was tired and needed to rest. Her breathing was very rapid.

As I drove Marie home, my little sister just kept talking about Kathleen's reaction. Marie was insistent they knew McGill.

I had to agree, it did seem a very strange reaction. Kathleen's lifelong habit over the years had been one of avoidance when she felt uncomfortable or didn't want to talk about something. She would distract you or shut down. It seemed an odd reaction to her sister asking an innocent question.

That was the last time Marie saw Kathleen alive. She still insists to this day McGill was known to Christopher and Kathleen. This theory was on my mind a lot.

I thought back to the trial and police saying McGill was a stranger to the area. Why did he choose to visit Partick then? What drew him there all the way from Edinburgh?

Remember this was in 1984. We didn't have a super connected transport system in those days. Maybe one bus a day, two tops between the two major cities. An hour long journey if not longer if the bus was stopping. Why did he take this time when he was on a limited freedom pass? It was his last two days of freedom.

I could not settle. After the trial, the crime scene photos were released to the press. I found myself looking at them on the internet. A shiver went through me when I saw the state of Mum's flat but one thing caught my eye. The domino table was set up, her fritters she'd bought that night were lying on the sofa open but untouched and her shoes were lying on the floor beside the sofa as if she'd just kicked them off her feet.

The police had said they believed Mum was dead within an hour or so of arriving home.

Kathleen had told me once that Mum had asked her to join her in the pub to play dominoes but she'd said no, she wanted to go home. But she was in the pub that night, she'd given a statement saying she'd left early.

So who was mum playing dominoes with? Herself? I keep coming back to the fact she wouldn't have let anyone in her house she didn't know. Did he follow her and force his way in? There weren't any signs of that according to the police.

Why did Kathleen ask Christopher to lie about her whereabouts between 11pm and 1am? At the very time my mum was likely dying.

What was she doing? Back then, shops weren't open at that time so she couldn't have been shoplifting. She was almost certainly doing something she didn't want the police to know about.

When I asked her about Christopher's claims, she would get angry and say his drug-addled brain was confused. But was it? I think back to my nephew and his tormented soul. He always blamed his mum. Was his torment really guilt? Had he unwittingly introduced his granny to a killer?

Kathleen and my mum spent at least every second day together but it is stuck in my brain that between 26 September and 2 October, when Martin found Mum, that Kathleen didn't see Mum and didn't mention to anyone any concerns she had about Mum's whereabouts. A full six days she didn't attempt to see Mum or ask if anyone else had seen her. I find that odd.

I couldn't rest. I had to speak to someone.

At the first meeting with the Procurator Fiscal after the trial I was still mentally unprepared and didn't really engage much with what was being said. Everyone else seemed satisfied with the outcome.

McGill's sentencing hearing came along in April 2021. He was sentenced to life imprisonment with a fixed punishment of 14 years. That is the minimum he would serve and after that it would be up to the parole board to decide if he was still a risk to the public and assess whether he could be freed or not. Considering he was 58 when he was convicted, he will be in his 70s before he is released.

Lord Burns made the following statement to the court:

"36 years after the death of Mary McLaughlin, you have been convicted of her murder. She was 58 when she died and you were 22. You are now 59. Her family has had to wait all that time in order to discover who was responsible for that act knowing that whoever did it was probably at large in the community. They had never given up the hope that someday they would find out what had happened to her. They have been deprived of her love and companionship.

"It is due to the perseverance of police authorities, and in particular the forensic biologists, that your guilt could be demonstrated.

"The evidence showed that your chance encounter with Mary McLaughlin that night allowed you to take advantage of a vulnerable and lonely woman who was probably intoxicated. The attack took place within her own home to which she may have invited you. She was wholly unable to defend herself against any attack from someone like you. You proceeded to strangle her with a cord until she was dead. You then left her in her house. From the evidence of Suzanne Russell, to which I can have regard, it may be that you made a calculated decision to kill this woman. She was eventually found by one of her sons. You continue to deny any responsibility for your actions. You therefore show no remorse for this murder.

"In the light of the verdict of the jury I must sentence you to life imprisonment. I also require to fix the punishment part of that sentence which reflects the period which you will serve before being considered for release on licence. It must satisfy the requirements of retribution and deterrence, taking into account the seriousness of the offence, and your previous convictions while ignoring any period of confinement which may be necessary for the protection of the public.

"Your record shows that you have been convicted of serious sexual offences in the past. You murdered Mary McLauglin when on licence after being convicted of assault with intent to rape and rape in April 1981. Subsequent to this murder, you were convicted of assault with intent to rape in 1999 and received a Discretionary Life Sentence. The Social Work Report suggests these crimes were committed on women who you did not know and were opportunistic attacks similar to the current offence.

"You have not been convicted of any offence since your release on life licence in October 2008, a period of 12 years. I have regard to your age now and to the fact that you have been in employment in the past.

"In the light of these circumstances, I consider that the punishment part should be fixed at 14 years. That is the minimum period which you will serve. It will then be for the Parole Board to assess the risk you pose and decide whether or not you should be released at some point thereafter.

I will backdate that sentence to 5 December 2019."

His words 'chance meeting' jumped out at me. While I was pleased it would appear that given his age McGill is likely to never see freedom outside again I was still consumed by thoughts he didn't meet my mum by chance after all.

I've contemplated writing to McGill, visiting him even but something is holding me back. I am afraid. Afraid I will get the answers I seek but also afraid he will laugh in my face and revel in my grief.

And what would I do with those answers if I ever got them? Will they bring me closure? Even if he told me he knew my sister and nephew, what good would it do now? I'd be left with bitterness and regret that I didn't challenge both of them when they were alive.

Even if he did agree to see me, could I take the word of a man who wanted to kill a helpless defenceless woman just to know what it felt like? Only 14 years for taking a life. It feels cheap. It's a hollow victory – it makes no odds to me McGill will die in prison. He's not suffering. He's being fed and watered every day, his medical needs met. He's being shown compassion in punishment – more than he afforded my mum.

Closure. What a weak word for such a huge emotion. Closure is a fallacy. I don't think there is such a thing. I'm afraid that even with every question answered, I will never get over her death. It was not natural. It shouldn't have happened.

Maybe I'm afraid that if I stop searching, I will finally have to face my grief.

I want to rail at the Gods for leaving such torment. I want to move on and I try to, God knows I try, but I can't.

IS ANYBODY LISTENING?

Someone suggested to me the idea another person was involved was "all in my head" – this infuriated me. It was a general consensus within the family that this was the case. I accept I am the only one who has not let that go. I am not stupid. I just feel in my gut that so much information was missed out and not given to the police.

I accept and am eternally grateful the police put forward the best case they could but nothing will convince me they had all of the information.

I decided to request another meeting with the Crown Office. I had things they needed to clear up for me. It was suggested that if I had any further concerns, my first port of call should be Police Scotland.

For legal reasons I cannot share the correspondence between myself and the Crown Office but suffice to say when I put it to one person within that office the information I held, they admitted they had not been aware of that and if they'd known they might have approached the case differently.

I still had contact details for one of the officers who had worked on Mum's review case. I decided to get in touch with her.

Angela Gentles was a fine detective who I know was diligent and invested in Mum's case. She assured me that every possible angle had been investigated thoroughly and that they had been unable to find a link between

Christopher and McGill. I pointed out that Christopher was dead so who else could confirm whether or not they were friends?

I fully appreciate the police did everything they could but I still believed they didn't have the full picture then or now. I firmly believe Kathleen, Christopher and McGill crossed paths with each other in 1984 prior to my mum's murder. Kathleen, when she was alive, remained stubbornly quiet on the issue. My only regret is now I didn't push harder.

If I am right, Kathleen would've spent many years terrified of the truth coming out. Perhaps a lot of her manner and behaviour and antics throughout her life was driven by guilt. I am not saying my sister killed my mother, but I do believe she introduced Mum to the man who took her life.

Perhaps she had suffered enough, I thought. Especially in her last few days.

I made the decision not to pursue it any further based on Kathleen's health at the time and the fact that Police Scotland and the legacy Strathclyde Police force had spent so much time and resources on Mum's case already that it was highly unlikely they would allocate more.

I reasoned that more recent murders had to take priority and I would just have to live with the questions for the rest of my life.

The Scottish Government decided in 2023 they were going to reform Scotland's Justice System, which has long been regarded as one of the best in the world.

Their new bill, which is still at the time of writing in the early stages, proposes to overhaul the system to make improvements that would benefit victims and their families.

Having been through this system it is often very cold, very bureaucratic and geared towards the criminals more than the people who have suffered.

As part of the consultation process the Scottish Government has set up a Taskforce which will use the experiences and ideas from those who have been through the criminal justice system to set about making changes for the better – providing parliament agrees.

I was invited by Victim Support Scotland to take part in workshops regarding the proposed Victims, Witnesses and Justice (Scotland) Bill. I was delighted to accept as I felt it was important to raise awareness about the impact crime has on victims. While I have received fantastic help from Victim Support there were limited resources and not everyone had the same experience I had.

I'm very much in favour of ongoing support for as long as necessary to help victims recover from their ordeal and what better example than myself who is still suffering more than 40 years on. You can never forget but you do eventually learn to live with it. Victims must never be left to pick up the pieces of their broken lives and shattered families themselves. It's a situation nobody asks to be in.

Under the current laws it feels like the perpetrators of crimes have many rights while the victims do not. When a murder is committed, life should mean life. There should be no parole for someone who has taken another person's life. I firmly believe sentences shouldn't be backdated either – after all, crime victims can't get their lives backdated can they?

My mum was killed by a man who, on day release, had been well-behaved before his parole. Training For Freedom, they said. He used that 'freedom' to take another life. If the justice system is serious about rehabilitating sex offenders and murderers then any training programme must be done 'in-house' and supervised. We've all read and seen stories where prisoners on parole or out on day trips commit more crimes.

Graham McGill is being treated very well inside. My view is, if you commit a serious crime, only your most basic needs should be met. Water, a bed to sleep in and basic food. That's it. You forfeit the right to luxuries and mollycoddling when you take another person's life. Perhaps my views are harsh but I would challenge anyone to give me a different view as long as they have been through it themselves. Until someone has lived experience they cannot possibly truly understand what it feels like to lose someone in that way.

I am 71 now. My mother died when I was 30. For 41 years I, and my siblings, have lived with the pain of her untimely death and suffered the consequences of that while her killer was out enjoying life and regretting nothing.

For justice reforms to really make a difference, the opinions, thoughts and feelings of victims and their families must be heard first.

23

Letting Go And Embracing New Beginnings

IT IS now 2025. I have exhausted every avenue open to me for over 40 years. I can do no more.

Just as the police said they left no stone unturned in the hunt for my mother's murderer, I have done the same to the best of my ability.

With both Kathleen and Christopher dead the opportunity to ask them again is gone. I'm aware that I had over 30 years to confront Kathleen and put her on the spot but sometimes you have to leave things and let them be and accept things for how they are. I can't live in regret for the things I did or didn't say.

Rightly or wrongly that's what I decided to do. I don't think my sister would've confessed. If she was ever going to tell the truth about her movements that night or if she knew McGill, the moment to do that had passed long before she died. The religious side of me believes that she will have to answer to a higher being than us. I hope so.

I still believe there is more to my mother's murder than we will ever know and I've accepted I will go to my own grave never knowing the full story. I've come to terms with that. I have no choice really.

I accept that her story was overly complex and with the passage of time many people have passed away and memories have dulled. I do not hold the police responsible for any failings – either in 1984 or in recent investigations.

It sometimes irritates and distresses me that I had to track down Mum's case files myself as the many times I went to the police, they had no record of her. Perhaps when Police Scotland was set up and all the files were centralised, things were different. I can only be grateful for that and hope that over time they have learned that while cases may be 'cold' to them, they are never as such to relatives.

Graham McGill deprived me of a reconciliation with my mother. Just as we were beginning to reconnect, she was taken away from me again. I miss what I never had. I will never know what it feels like to be cocooned in the love of your mother. And that is a pain that will stay with me until I draw my last breath.

My mother's murder has dominated all of my adult life. When this book closes, I am hoping it will finally help lay my demons to rest and I can live the rest of my life, however long that may be, with a semblance of peace.

I'm aware that parts of the book come across as self indulgent and being one child out of 11, it isn't completely MY story but I can only recount the story as was my experience of it. My siblings may have their own accounts and thoughts and feelings and I have by no means spoken for them. I'm sure they all have their own memories of Mum.

For me personally, it felt and still feels important to me to get my mum's story out there – the real story of who she was and how her brutal murder impacted her family.

I think after reading this book you can see the domino effect one death can have on a family, on a person. So much tragedy has befallen our family. I hope now that some semblance of justice has been served, we may finally know peace.

A few months after Kathleen died I decided to close down an old email account which hadn't been used in several years. I was about to hit delete when I noticed amongst the spammers and marketing emails were two that looked like they were from genuine people.

LETTING GO AND EMBRACING NEW BEGINNINGS

Opening the first one I was blown away when I realised it was from my mum's first cousin, Fay, and another from her niece Karen. They had been trying to get in contact with me since 2021. They now live in Canada and America and were able to tell me a bit more about Mum which was amazing. I discovered I have relatives living all over the world and I'm hoping to be in touch with some of them in the near future.

As for my future, I'm not sure how much longer that will be, but I finally feel free. I have done all I can for Mum. My future is to live my life with my children, grandchildren, great grandchild, and have as much quality time as God allows me. Whether that be holidays together or family celebrations I plan to just spend as much time with them as I can.

They have been on this journey with me. They deserve my full attention at last. I have written some children's easy to learn English books that I have had sitting on the backburner for a long time.

My daughter, Laura, is a talented artist and I'm hoping she will be able to do illustrations for me and then I hope to publish them and target the foreign market.

This life, or rather the murder, has taken its toll on all of us.

Graham McGill didn't just rob my mother of her life, he took all of ours. Her children. Our lives were destroyed by his actions. 14 years seems cheap for all of the lives he took that night.

Maybe if I have enough fight left in me, changing the laws will be my next mission. I believe my faith in God is what got me through this life. As far as I'm concerned, Judgement Day comes to us all.

On September 26, 1984, Mary 'Ginger Murphy' McLaughlin went out to have fun.

That night she met the devil himself and he took her life.

I always felt she was not at peace. I could feel her presence with me all the time. I did my best for her. I am done now.

I hope her story will last forever. I hope people will remember Wee Mary long after I'm gone. She deserves that much.

Acknowledgements

MY SINCERE thanks to everyone who made it possible to bring justice for "Wee Mary "and to those who I will be forever grateful.

Police Scotland Cold Case Team – without the dedication and tenacity of their hard work, the case might never have been solved. This includes DC Kenny McCubbin (Retired), Detective Superintendent Suzanne Chow, DC Angela Gentles.

I also want to extend my thanks and appreciation to the Crown Office and Procurator Fiscal Service and Alex Prentice KC for their help, assistance and bringing a successful prosecution. Also to the Family Liaison Team from that office who helped support us during a difficult time.

Forensic Scientist, Joanne Cochrane who worked tirelessly on my Mother's case and I appreciate her dedication and skill in ensuring my mother's killer could be identified.

My thanks must also go to Victim Support Service

for Scotland and Jane Hamilton Author and Journalist who have helped me more than they will ever know.

To Clare Fitzsimons, Christine Costello and Claire Brown at Mirror Books – you work hard and you've been amazing. Thank you.

And last but not least, my children who put up with a mother determined to find answers. Thank you.